iPhone 13 User Guide for Seniors

A Unique Book to Learn the First Steps to Take From the Moment You Get an iPhone in Your Hand, up to the Most Complex Things

Brandon Ballard

CONTENTS

INTRODUCTION

The iPhone 13 series is finally here, and Apple has sought to give its users the best money they can buy in all 4 of its variants. This ranges from the lower-priced smartphones, the iPhone 13 and iPhone 13 mini, to the higher-priced iPhone 13 Pro and iPhone 13 Pro max. All 4 models have many features set to blow you away and give you the best smartphone experience ever!

iPhone 13 offers a high level of user security with Face ID (easily the most secure smartphone authentication capability to unlock the device and make payments), a 12MP wide camera, a 12 MP ultra-wide shooter, and a 12 MP f/2.2 front selfie camera. The wide camera has an aperture of f/1.6, and the ultra-wide camera has an f/2.4 aperture. Night-mode photos on the new iPhone (47% more light) have way more detail and sensor-shift optical image stabilization for steady images. Also, there are new Photographic Styles.

The iPhone 13 is a next-generation iPhone with many impressive and advanced features. iPhone 13 is powered by the A15 Bionic chipset and the spectacular True Depth camera system for high-quality optics and photography. In addition, the device runs on the new iOS 16, packed with innovative updates to existing apps and the latest feature additions.

The iPhone features a flat-edge design with a Super Retina XDR display for a vivid viewing experience. Also, wireless charging, a dual-camera system with immense low-light photography capability, and a tough ceramic shield glass finish that is highly dust and water-resistant; protect the device from wear.

The iPhone 13 is a 5G-compatible device that includes a new 16-core Neural Engine capable of processing 15.8 trillion operations per second and offers all-in-one integration of top-notch hardware and software with faster streaming, downloads and multi-player gaming in real-time for exquisite user experience.

iPhone 13 has a 6.1-inch display with Apple's custom OLED technology. The design is beautiful, water-resistant, and durable while providing unmatched performance. In addition, a lithium-polymer battery powers the iPhone 13. It delivers up to 45 hours of audio playback and fast wireless charging.

A new, enhanced camera unit makes the iPhone 13 even better at photography. Its larger sensor significantly increases the details captured in every photo or video recording. It helps enhance low-light performance almost twice that of the standard iPhone 12. And with the new Cinematic Mode, Apple brings Hollywood-grade video recording capabilities to the iPhone for the first time.

The iPhone 13 has state-of-the-art video recording capabilities. Apple's latest flagship iPhones narrow the gulf between professional high-definition and smartphone cameras. It can capture, replay, and edit 10-bit High Dynamic Range (HDR) recording with the help of Dolby Vision technology.

If you apply it correctly, this book can only help you get the most out of your new iPhone 13 smartphone. Use this guidebook's various easy guides and explanations to explore the iPhone 13's many powerful functions. You will enjoy your device's numerous features and functions as you become more familiar with it. Thanks for getting the book and taking the time to read its content!

Phone 13 Top Features

Wireless Charging

Apple has included wireless charging on its latest smartphone; this implies it can get you a full charge by merely being positioned on a compatible wireless charging pad. The iPhone 13 uses the established Qi ecosystem; this means it will use most accessories on the marketplace.

A15 Bionic Processor

Apple's iPhone 13 was the fastest iPhone possible when it was introduced. The latest A15 Bionic chip has around 30% faster graphics performance than the prior processor in the iPhone 13. If true, it's much more likely to outperform its predecessor and all Android rivals introduced in 2017 and early 2018.

New Colors and Design

Apple has included some new colors around the iPhone 13, with the unit sale in space grey, gold, and silver. The iPhone 13 and iPhone 13 Plus also introduce a pleasant cup-back design. Don't worry about it breaking, as Apple says it's the most durable cup ever inside a smartphone.

It employs a 7-layer color process for precise hue and opacity, delivering a rich depth of color using a color-matched aerospace-grade aluminum bezel. The iPhone 13 and iPhone 13 Plus will also be water- and dust-resistant.

Extra Storage

There's the good news if you're constantly monitoring storage space, as Apple has included 64GB as standard. That's double the virtual memory within the iPhone 13. Apple, furthermore, offers ditched the 128GB version using the iPhone 13 featuring 256GB of in-built storage.

It's also worth noting that iOS 14, which launches in just a few months, will automatically reduce the size of photos taken for the iPhone's camera, providing users with a lot more extra space.

Powerful Picture Editing

The iPhone 13 features Apple's powerful fresh A15 Bionic processor and an improved camera. These characteristics make the iPhone 13 an excellent tool, even for professional photographers. The App Store includes a vast range of photo editing apps. Using the proper apps, you can create your photos to look superb and professional. Among my favorites is Photofox. It combines the simplicity of mobile editing and enhancement using the vigor and countless top features of desktop apps, such as Adobe Photoshop.

The app allows you to edit images in levels, which may significantly function in professional picture editing. In addition, creating unique designs with visual elements is straightforward. The application form is usually free but contains in-app purchases.

Portraits with Portrait Lighting

Apple introduced the wonderful Face photo setting in the iPhone 13 Plus. However, the iPhone 13 Plus must go to another level with Face Lighting.

In brief, Face photo mode offers razor-sharp portrait photos of the subject matter having a blurry background. However, the iPhone 13 Plus allows you to add unique lighting like a studio. The most effective part is that once you've taken an image using Portrait mode, you can change the lighting settings afterward to make your picture appear as you intended.

You can customize the light settings from the portrait photograph you already took by tapping Edit in the preview in the Photos app. The Face Lighting wheel should appear, which you can slide to improve the image configurations.

Screen Recording

The newest iPhones include native screen recording built-in - there's no reliance on third-party apps; this new feature is now available in the iPhone's Control Centre, which you can access by swiping up from the bottom of the screen. Unfortunately, the display documenting icon isn't in the Control Centre by default; you must add it to the iPhone's configurations/settings page.

The iPhone 13 and iPhone 13 Mini

The iPhone 13 and iPhone 13 Mini are 2 smartphone models produced, designed, and marketed by Apple Inc. They are the 15th generation, lower-cost iPhones developed as a successor to the iPhone 12. On September 14, 2021, they were unveiled in a virtually organized Apple Special Event at Apple Park in Cupertino, California, alongside the pricy iPhone 13 Pro and iPhone 13 Pro Max flagships. Apple also made the iPhone 13 and 1Phone 13 mini smartphones available for pre-order on the 17th of September 2021, and they went on sale on September 24, 2021.

At first glance, the iPhone 13 smartphone does not appear to be new. It has a remarkably similar design to the iPhone 12, with a flat frame consistent with Apple's recent models. It could lead to many people labeling it as a minor update. However, this is not the case, as we'll see soon.

It has a few variations, including slightly lower button placement, Face ID, and a True Depth sensor compared to its predecessors. It also has larger rear cameras positioned diagonally, with a notch that is 20 times smaller, even though most users have a weird conflicting relationship with this feature. However, as you start to use this frontline smartphone, you'll realize that it offers much more than just a smaller but taller speaker notch, with a beautiful, brighter display than any of its precursors.

The battery life has been extended. In addition, Apple has made massive improvements to an already great camera with a feature known as computational photography that gives you that professional feel when using the camera. There is also a larger storage capacity, not forgetting the A15 bionic chip, the fastest chip globally; yes, you read that right. So now, let's get right into the specs.

iPhone 13 Mini

If you thought small-sized phones were dead, I'm sorry to disappoint you because, with the iPhone 13 Mini leading the charge, pocket-sized phones are not going away anytime soon. Regardless of the size, the iPhone 13 Mini is stellar in itself. Some have even referred to it as the most powerful small phone ever. That's quite a big claim to slap on a phone, but maybe you'll see why later.

While Apple has saved a few standout features for the iPhone 13 Pro and iPhone 13 Pro Max, the iPhone 13 Mini receives many welcome improvements. These are a brighter display, a faster A15 Bionic processor, and fascinating new camera features like Cinematic mode for video.

Unboxing iPhone 13, iPhone 13 Mini, iPhone 13 Pro, and iPhone 13 Pro Max

The unboxing experience is the same for all iPhone 13s. The iPhone 13, iPhone 13 mini, iPhone 13 Pro, and iPhone 13 Pro Max all come in light boxes because the package has no power brick. Apple also removed the plastic shrink-wrap from the iPhone 13s, which it claims has helped save up to 600 metric tons of plastic.

Apple now uses many recycled materials in its aluminum case and cardboard box for zero waste. The accessories that come with the package are mostly the same. You get lightning to USB-C cable, a SIM card tool, a white Apple sticker, and a manual.

GETTING STARTED WITH IPHONE 13

We'll cover the basics of turning the iPhone on, off and restarting the iPhone before launching into setup.

Turn Your Device On

- Hold down the right side button until the Apple logo shows.

- If your iPhone doesn't power on, you may need to charge the battery before trying again.

Switch iPhone Off

- iPhone with Face ID: Press the side button and hold both volume buttons simultaneously until the display of the slider is shown, then drag the Power Off slider down.

- Home button iPhone: Press and hold a side button (depending on your preference) and drag the slider. Sleep/Wake button.

- **Illustrations of 3 iPhone models, all facing screens:** On the left side of the gadget, the picture depicts the up and down volume buttons. The side button on the right is displayed. The center picture shows the side button on the right side of the gadget. The graphic on the top of the smartphone depicts the Sleep/Wake button.

- All models: Enter Settings > click General > press shut down, then drag the slider.

Force Restart

- Do the following:

  ○ Press the volume up button, and release it fast.

○ Next, press and hold down the side button. Release the button if the Apple logo is displayed.

An example of an iPhone model face up without a Home button. Instead, on the left side of the gadget, the up and down volume controls are displayed, and on the left side, a second button is shown.

Charging Your iPhone

The iPhone is fitted with a lithium-ion rechargeable battery that is light, charges fast, and has a long life.

It is important to ensure the device is charging so that it does not shut down unexpectedly or run out of battery during the **Setup** process.

Remove the film material around the power adapter. The film is intended as a protective cover around the adapter to prevent damage.

Next, the AC plug with the USB cable should be inserted into a power outlet and the other end of the cable should be inserted into the power adapter port of the iPhone. (Ensure the power ratings of the plug and the power outlet are compatible to avoid damaging the device).

You can also charge the iPhone wirelessly with a Qi-certified charger (available as an accessory at Apple stores).

- Connect the charger to a power source and place the iPhone on the charger face up and wait for a few seconds for it to start charging. For s smooth experience, remove any casings from the iPhone and ensure that there is no barrier between it and the Qi-certified charger. The iPhone models that support wireless charging are iPhone 8, iPhone 8 Plus, iPhone X, iPhone XS, iPhone XS Max, iPhone XR, iPhone Pro Max, iPhone Pro, iPhone SE (second generation), iPhone 11, iPhone 12, iPhone 12 mini, iPhone 12 Pro and iPhone 12 Pro Max, iPhone 13.

The battery charge status icon at the top right corner of the screen indicates the battery level and charging status. A battery charging icon shows that the device is well connected to the AC source. The battery charges faster when the device is off or in a sleep mode. Once the battery is fully charged, please remove the cable and disconnect the AC plug from the power outlet.

For optimal usage of the battery and to conserve the battery power, disconnect any accessories connected to the iPhone that are not in use, reduce the display brightness and close any unused apps.

iPhone Setup

Your brand new iPhone is ready for you to set up right out of the box. A nice "Hello" will welcome you.

From this stage, you will be able to customize your iPhone as if it were new or move your data from another phone, like an Android or Windows phone. Do not worry; we will walk you through it all.

You can setup your iPhone 13 in one of three ways

1. setup as new

2. restore from another iPhone

3. import content from a non-Apple phone.

Here's what each of those choices means in more depth

Setup as new means starting from scratch (assume the phone is completely new and doesn't have any of your information). This is for people who have never before used a smartphone or online services or who want a completely brand new feel with their iPhone.

Restore from a previous iPhone, iPad, or iPod touch backup. This can be accomplished with iCloud online or iTunes or Finder (macOS Catalina) over USB. This is for those who had a previous iOS device and are switching to a new one and want the new one to be setup with all the contacts and other settings they had on the older device.

Importing from Android, BlackBerry, or Windows Phone - To make Android simpler; Apple has a Google Play app, but online services allow you to transfer a lot of data from any old mobile. This is for individuals moving from a different mobile device to an iPhone or iPad.

The moment you turn your new iPhone on for the first time, in many languages, you will be greeted with "Hello." If you start from scratch, restore from a different iPhone, or turn from Android, it's the same.

1. To get started, touch the slide and slide your finger across the screen.

2. Select your language.

3. Select your country or region.

4. Select a network with Wi-Fi. You can choose to set up later if you are not in Wi-Fi network range. Instead, pick Cellular. (More details on how to set up your iPhone with Wi-Fi will be discussed extensively later in the book). Either a Wi-Fi or Cellular network is required for setup. At this point, you can choose to set up your new iPhone with the same passcode and settings as another iPhone using Automatic Setup. If you want to manually set up your new iPhone, continue with the steps below.

5. After reading about the Data & Privacy details for Apple, tap Proceed.

6. Tap Allow Services for Venue. Select Skip Location Services if you don't want to allow localization services at this time. You can manually activate such location services, including Maps.

Inserting the Sim and Setting up Mobile Data Plan

A SIM is required to access Cellular and data services when connected to a GSM or CDMA network. The iPhone uses a nano-SIM.

Certain functions and capabilities of the iPhone would not be functional until a wireless network is available. You may need to contact your preferred wireless service provider for more details regarding roaming, availability of access, restrictions, and policy governing the wireless service.

To Insert the Nano-SIM

1. Insert a SIM ejector pin into the hole of the SIM tray and push forward.

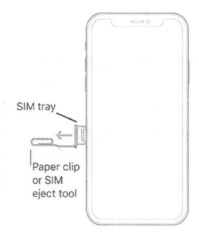

1. The SIM tray will pop-out and can be removed from the iPhone.

2. Put the SIM into the SIM tray in a way that it aligns with the shape of the SIM tray.

3. Place the tray back gently into the space from which it was ejected in the iPhone.

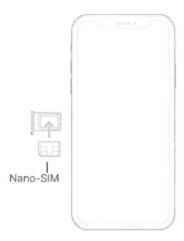

Nano-SIM

You can activate a mobile data plan on your iPhone including a roaming arrangement (depending on the network provider's policy). Do this by navigating to Settings > Mobile Data and follow the prompts.

Set up Assistant

The setup assistant is auto-activated. The setup assistant was built as a walkthrough guide for the first steps required to use the iPhone. To select, click, double click and move items around on the screen, use the touch screen.

Choose your **Country** and click **Continue**. You can change this later by navigating to **Settings > Language and Region**.

Next, pick the **Keyboard** layout of your choice and click **Continue**. Choose your network type (Wi-Fi, Ethernet, or none and click continue). Select your preferred Internet Protocol (IP) from the connection type list and enter the IP address, subnet mask, default gateway, and DNS server address in the required fields and then click **Continue**. If there are available Wi-Fi networks available, just select your Wi-Fi network and enter the passcode to connect to the Internet through the network.

Apple's Data and Privacy Information will be displayed on the screen. The information would help you understand how Apple makes use of the data it collects from you as you use the iPhone especially in terms of product improvement and research focused on future updates. Read through the information and click **Continue**.

To transfer information to this device, select the correct option from the available options like iPhone, iPhone, iPhone touch, or Android device. If you do not have existing data to transfer (setting up the iPhone for the first time) or would prefer to do this later, select the option **Don't Transfer Any Information Now**.

Enter your Apple ID in the required field, click **Continue** and input the corresponding password. If you do not already have an Apple ID, you can create one during this set-up. After getting an Apple ID, you can then sign in to your device. The Apple ID is very important, and it requires an email address and a password. Just one Apple ID is required to use any Apple Service and it is best practice not to share the details with anyone. Apple ID is the account that will enable you to get the most out of your Apple devices—including downloading apps from the App Store, Siri, buying music and movies from iTunes Store, pushing and storing content in iCloud and other Apple resources.

If the password you entered is correct, you will be automatically signed into apps and services that require Apple ID. If you do not remember your Apple ID password, click on the 'Forgot Apple ID or password?' link that is available in the sign-in window for the recovery of the password.

The Terms and Conditions window contains license terms for using the Apple device that you need to read and click **Agree**.

Input all the compulsory fields and then click on Create a Computer Account window and then Continue.

Congratulations! You have created a new user account with which you can log into your iPhone with admin rights allowing you to download and install apps, create other user accounts and make system changes.

Next, configure your device with frequently used settings by clicking Continue on the Express Setup window. This takes you to the Home Screen page and the setup is complete.

Sign in with Your Apple ID

- If you did not log in during configuration, do the following:

- Go to **Settings**.

- Tap **Sign in to your iPhone**.

- Enter your Apple ID and password.

- If you do not have an Apple ID, you can create one.

- To protect your account with 2-factor authentication, enter the six-digit verification code.

If you forget your Apple ID or password, see Recovering Your Apple ID.

A free iCloud account is part of your Apple ID. iCloud provides a free email account and 5GB of storage for emails, documents, photos and videos, and backups. Purchased music, apps, TV shows, and books are not included in the available storage. You can update your iCloud storage directly from the iPhone.

Note: Some iCloud features have minimum system requirements. The availability of iCloud and its services varies by country and region.

SETUP FACE ID

The Face ID setup is identical to the Touch ID setup, except simpler. As part of your initial iPhone setup, iOS will offer to let you set up a Face ID. But if you skipped it at setup, you can set up Face ID whenever you like or reset it.

1. Open up **Settings** from your home screen.
2. Click the **Passcode & Face ID**.
3. Input your passcode.
4. Click Set up Face ID (or Set up Alternative Appearance if Face ID has already been set up).
5. Click the Get Started button.

6. Perform the first scan by turning your head slowly in a circle.
7. Click **Continue**
8. Perform the second scan by turning the head slowly in a circle.

1. Click **Done**

You can now begin to use Face ID on your new iPhone 13!

- During the Face ID setup, you can choose Accessibility Options if you have physical restrictions. Setting up face recognition in this manner only necessitates using part of the range of head movements. Face ID is still safe, but it necessitates a more consistent approach to how you look at your iPhone.

- If you're blind or have limited eyesight, Face ID includes an accessibility option you may utilize. If you don't want Face ID to need you to look at your iPhone with your eyes open, go to Settings > Accessibility and turn off Require Attention for Face ID. Additionally, if you use VoiceOver when you initially set up your iPhone, this function is disabled.

Disable Face ID

You may block Face ID from unlocking your iPhone for a limited time.

- Hold down the side button for 2 seconds and any volume icon.

- When the slider is displayed, click the side button to lock the iPhone immediately.

- Your iPhone will automatically lock if you don't touch the screen for a minute.

- Face ID will be activated again the next time you unlock your iPhone with your passcode.

- Face ID should be turned off.

- Go to settings > Face ID and Passcode.

- Choose one of the following options:

  ○ Face ID may be turned off for particular services only: Turn off iPhone Unlock, Apple Pay, iTunes, App Store, Safari AutoFill, or all of them.

  ○ Turn off Face ID by resetting it.

  ○ If your iPhone is lost or stolen, you may use Find My iPhone Lost Mode to prevent Face ID from being used to unlock it.

Turn off Face ID "Require Attention"

By default, your iPhone with Face ID support enabled will require you to look at it and that your eyes are open before it is authenticated. If you want to be able to unlock it without looking directly at your iPhone screen, you can turn it off for reasons of usability or convenience. It's not as safe, but you can do it if you want to unlock your iPhone while it's on the table or if you're keeping it sideways.

Note: In order to authenticate you, the Face ID device also needs to be able to see your eyes, nose, and mouth. But there's a limit to its field of view, even with the attention off.

If you don't want to turn on iPhone's gaze detection feature:

1. Go to **Settings** > **Face ID and Passcode**.

2. Enable or disable the following options:

- Require to look toward Face ID.

- Attention Aware Features.

- Haptic feedback with successful authentication

If you enable VoiceOver during the first iPhone setup, these settings are turned off by default.

How to Reset Face ID

If you want to change the face of the person that is registered on your iPhone or you just want to redo your Face ID setup for whatever reason, you can!

Note: No confirmation is needed; dear Apple, add a confirmation dialog, please! Your face ID will be gone the moment you press the button, and you'll be required to set it up again to get Face ID back.

1. Go to **Settings** > **Face ID and Passcode**.

2. Do one of the following:

- Disable Face ID for specific items only: disable one or more of the options-"Unlock iPhone," "Apple Pay," "iTunes and App Store," or "Autofill Safari."

- Disable Face ID: tap "Setup Face ID."

KNOW YOUR SETTINGS

The following paragraphs discuss various settings you can update on your iPhone 13 to improve its responsiveness and the overall user experience. There are several settings in your iPhone 13, so it helps to play around with your device a little until you get used to it. This is a brief overview to show you some of the possible things with your new iPhone, but there's a lot more about your device you can figure out on your own.

Personal Information

Right at the top of the settings screen, you will see your name along with your Apple ID. If you tap on that, you will be able to reset your Apple ID and change some things about your iCloud and iTunes accounts.

Underneath your name, there's the Airplane Mode, Wi-Fi, Bluetooth, and Cellular. These are all features you can access from the Control Center, which you can open by swiping downwards from your screen's top right corner.

Notifications Settings

Right below this panel are the notifications. If you tap the notifications settings open, you will see the Show Previous option, which controls when and how notifications are displayed.

If you tap on the Show Previous option, you will see three choices to pick from: Always, When Unlocked, and Never. If you select Show Previous Always, you will always see previous notifications on the Lock Screen. If you choose Show Previous When Unlocked, no notification will be displayed until your iPhone is unlocked. Finally, if you select the Show Previous Never option, then your device will not display notifications whether it is locked or unlocked. As a recommendation, choose the "Show Previous When Unlocked" option, as one will have to unlock your iPhone before they can view your notifications.

Do Not Disturb settings

The **Do Not Disturb** settings in the **Settings→ Focus** section control all the **Do Not Disturb** feature configurations, which helps to put your device in silent mode when you don't want interference caused by incoming calls, messages, and other notification sounds. Open **Settings** then select **Focus** to open these settings. In the Do Not Disturb settings screen, you can also schedule when the feature becomes active and when it comes off automatically. For instance, you can schedule the Do Not Disturb feature to become active at 10 PM during bedtime and turn it off by 7 AM. You can allow calls and texts from certain people by adding them to the People section so that you don't miss an emergency call.

General settings

You can update your operating system (OS) from the **General** settings in the Settings app. To do this, tap on **General** in the settings app, and then tap on **Software Update**.

There are a few additional options in the General settings screen that may be helpful. Scroll down the **General Settings** screen to find the i**Phone Storage** option. This contains vital information about how much storage space all the different apps in your iPhone are taking up. It also gives you the option of getting rid of any app you feel is not useful but is consuming a sizable amount of your storage space.

You can also customize the keyboard under the **Keyboards** item and set usage restrictions for specific files and applications from the general settings.

One very useful section of the **General** settings is **Background App Refresh**. This shows which apps are continuing to run even if you aren't viewing them on the screen. If you want to get notifications or updates, the app needs to run in the background (think of mapping using Maps, etc) but if you don't need the app to run, turn the background refresh for an app off to save battery life.

Display & Brightness settings

Just below **General** in the settings app is the **Display & Brightness** settings. In this settings screen, you can adjust your display's brightness, modify the size of the texts shown on your display, decide how long your display should stay on without activity before auto-locking, etc.

Sounds and Haptics

The **Sounds and Haptics** settings allow you to change your phone sounds (ringtones, message tones, etc.), while Haptics deals with your iPhone's vibration behavior.

Check for Software Updates

Once the setup is completed, go to the **Home** screen and click on **App Store**. Select the circle in the upper right corner with your initials in it. This takes you to your **Account** screen. Scroll down and you'll see a section allowing you to install any available software updates for your installed Apps. You can begin to use your iPhone once your software is up to date.

Settings Search on iPhone

1. Tap **Settings** on the Home screen (or app library).

2. At the top of the screen is a search bar that you can use to quickly find a setting. Enter a term such

as "iCloud," and then tap the **search** button on the lower right of the keyboard (normally labelled as Enter on the keyboard).

Move Data from Old to New iPhone

If you did not transfer files from your old device during configuration, you will need to use a 3rd party tool for the transfer. Do the following:

<u>Step 1:</u>

1. Download and install Anytrans on the computer.

2. Open it and connect the iPhones to the computer using USB cables.

3. Choose the "Phone Switcher."

4. Click on "Phone to iPhone" mode.

<u>Step 2:</u>

1. Choose the device from which the info is to be transferred and place it in the new device

2. Click the "Next" button to continue. It helps you transfer data from Android and iPhone to your new iPhone at the same time.

<u>Step 3:</u>

1. Select file categories to transfer.

2. Click "Next" button to move data from the old iPhone to the new iPhone.

Tips: Besides, you can also go to the category management screen to preview first and then select the data you want to transfer.

Wake and Unlock iPhone

The iPhone turns off the screen to save power, locks itself for security, and goes to sleep when you're not using it. You can quickly wake up and unlock your iPhone when you want to use it again. The iPhone will lock automatically if you don't touch the screen for about a minute.

Wake up iPhone

Do one of the following to activate iPhone:

- Touch the side button or the sleep/sleep button.

- Pick up the iPhone. You can turn off Raise to turn on in Settings> Display & brightness.

- Touch the screen

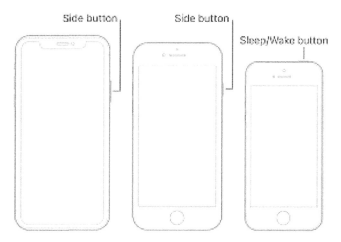

Unlock iPhone with Face ID

1. Touch the screen or lift the iPhone to wake it up, and then glance at your iPhone.

2. The lock symbol moves from off to open (unlock) to show that the iPhone is opened.

3. Slide up from the base (bottom) of the screen.

4. Press the side button to re-lock iPhone. iPhone locks automatically if you don't touch the screen for about a minute.

Unlock iPhone with Touch ID

1. On an iPhone with a home button, press the home button with your finger that you enrolled with Touch ID.

2. Press the side button or the sleep/wake button (depending on your model) to re-lock iPhone. iPhone locks automatically if you don't touch the screen for about a minute.

Unlock iPhone with a Password

1. Slide up from the base (bottom) of the lock screen (on an iPhone with Face ID) or tap down the Home button (on other iPhone models).

2. Enter the passcode (if you have set the iPhone to require a passcode).

3. Press the side button or sleep/wake button (depending on your model) to re-lock iPhone. iPhone locks automatically if you don't touch the screen for about a minute.

Change iPhone's Language

With the iPhone 12, users can access the Apple application store to purchase various games, utilities, and ringtones.

Some users who speak other languages may have difficulty finding their way through the app store as the default language is English.

However, users can change the language to one that they are comfortable with.

1. Open the **Settings** app from the Home screen. The **Settings** app has an icon that appears like two gears moving together.

2. Scroll down and tap **General** which also looks like a gear icon.

3. Scroll down until you see the **Language and Region** option and click on it.

4. Under **Preferred Languages**, select **Add Language** and scroll through the options to choose the best match or type in the Search bar at the top. Choose your desired language. A check will appear close to the language you chose.

5. Press the "Home" button to return to the home screen. When you open the app store, the new language will appear.

How to Customize VoiceOver

Voiceover can recognize a lot of different things on display now. It uses on-device intelligence to recognize elements on your screen to improve overall support.

1. Go to VoiceOver Recognition

2. Turn ON (or OFF) Image Descriptions and Screen Recognition

3. Turning ON Image Description and Screen Recognition allows your phone to explain anything you tap on and things on your display. Screen recognition will detect everything from interface

controls to aid in navigating apps.

How to Adjust Ringtone Volume

You can adjust the ringer volume on your iPhone via Settings or the volume button on the side of your device.

Via Settings

1. Open the **Settings** app, then go to **Sounds & Haptics**.

2. Drag the slider under **Ringtone and Alert Volume** to adjust the volume level.

Via Volume Buttons

1. First, go to **Settings**, then go to **Sounds & Haptics**.

2. Scroll to **Ringtone and Alert Volume,** turn on **Change with Buttons**.

If you enable this feature, the volume buttons will now have two functions:

- Ringer and alerts function when you are not using media.

- Controls media volume when watching a video or listening to music.

An Unresponsive Phone

If your phone is totally unresponsive, don't panic. Quickly tap the volume up button, then the volume down button, then press and hold the side power button until the Apple logo appears. This will reset the iPhone.

How to Turn the Device Off and On Again

Simultaneously hold down the *Volume Up* button and the *Side* buttons for few seconds.

- Slide the onscreen power symbol at the top to the right.

- Once the iPhone power off, hold the side button until the Apple logo appears to turn it back on.

This method carries out a graceful shutdown followed by the usual turn-on process. I recommend trying to use this method to solve the issue first.

How to Force Restart

Quickly press and release the volume up button, followed by the volume down button.

Hold down the side button and release it when the Apple logo appears.

Although this method will try to restart your device, the issue might not actually be resolved. If the iPhone does not turn back on, Apple's support pages give more tips, including how to recover the device in more serious cases.

Note: When restarting your device, make sure to pay attention and follow all instructions properly. Specifically make sure not to confuse the restart instructions and end up holding down the up volume and side buttons for a long time. In doing so, the Emergency SOS feature will begin a five-second countdown, where it will count down from five and vibrate with each number as the Emergency SOS slider fills up. If the counter gets to 0 and you are still holding both buttons down, your phone will consider the bar full and dial the emergency services, which may inform the police or an ambulance of your location. Just pay attention and if the vibration and countdown begin, release the buttons.

How to Update iOS

iOS is the Operating System of the iPhone. The operating system is the software that recognizes the button presses, open apps, and is the coordinator of everything that goes on in the iPhone.

1. Go to **Settings > General > Software Update**.

2. Tap "**Download and Install.**"

3. Tap on **Install** to update. Or you can select **Later** and tap on **Install Tonight** or **Remind Me Later**. If you select **Install Tonight**, plug your device into power before you go to bed. Your device will automatically update overnight. Enter your passcode if you are asked to.

To turn automatic updates on:

1. Head to **Settings**, then to **General**, and then tap on **Software Update**

2. Customize **Automatic Updates**, then turn on **Install iOS Updates.**

Emoji Search

To easily find the perfect expressions, this is perfect. Tap the emoji icon on your keyboard to use this feature, and you'll see a new emoji search field at the top of it.

Keyboard Updates

The iOS 14 keyboard has device dictation. The keyboard will also display autofill suggestions from contacts, email addresses, phone numbers, and more.

There are new dictionaries for French, German, Indonesian, English, Japanese, simplified Chinese, and Polish English. There are also redesigned Japanese kana keyboards with easier input.

Set Up Wi-Fi, Bluetooth, and Mobile Data

Wi-Fi

- Launch the **Settings** app on your iPhone and select **Wi-Fi**.

- On the **Wi-Fi** page, at the top is the Wi-Fi switch for enabling/disabling Wi-Fi. Turn it on.

- Also on the **Wi-Fi** page, there is a section labelled **Networks**. Select the Wi-Fi network you want to connect to and enter the Password if required.

Bluetooth

Bluetooth pairing can be a little daunting but don't worry; once you know how it works, it's very easy to learn. Bluetooth pairing is the same process you use for any Bluetooth-enabled device—like a headset or Bluetooth speaker. However, this process includes a little set of instructions you need to follow.

To Turn On Bluetooth On

On your iPhone, go to **Settings** > **Bluetooth**. Turn Bluetooth on by choosing Bluetooth off.

If you want to be able to use both Wi-Fi and Bluetooth simultaneously, you will need to be connected to both networks at the same time. You will need to make sure the Bluetooth is turned on and paired. You can do this by selecting Bluetooth in the Wi-Fi settings. On iOS (iPhone and iPad), go to Settings > Bluetooth.

How to Pair Bluetooth Headphones

- Open the **Settings** app on your iPhone.

- Go to **Bluetooth**.

- Tap the Bluetooth headphone that you want to pair. You will see the Bluetooth button in blue.

- You will see a notification on your iPhone. Then you will see the Bluetooth headphones paired to your iPhone.

Mobile Data

Mobile data allows connecting to the internet only when it is required. Suppose there is data available in your cellular data plan. In that case, your internet use is not limited to Wi-Fi networks because you can use your cellular plan.

Turning on Cellular Data allows us to choose the network type that works better and requires fewer resources.

The data you will use depends on the location, how much data you need at a particular time and the speed you use. With this, iOS can make decisions based on network performance and your location.

How to Turn on Mobile Data

Now let's see the steps required to enable or turn on mobile data

- Open **Settings** -> **Cellular**. Note the **Cellular Data** switch, if you haven't enabled the feature, you will see an option to turn on the **Cellular Data**.

After you have turned on the cellular data, you will see the data usage on your cellular plan. On the last screen, you will see the data limit reached or the amount of data used.

If you've reached the maximum data limit, you will see an option to buy more data.

If you've exceeded your data plan, you will see an option to turn off the data.

The cellular data is turned off if you have reached the usage limit.

Turning off the cellular data will also remove this option from the **Cellular Data** settings.

How to Turn off Mobile Data

To turn off the cellular data, open **Settings** -> **Cellular** -> Turn off **Cellular Data**.

Here you will see an option to turn off cellular data. Suppose you tap on Turn off Cellular Data. In that case, it automatically turns off the cellular data and removes the usage notification.

APPLE ID

Apple ID Background

Apple ID is a unique id that is used in the setup of your iPhone. Since it is unique, it is the way that Apple uses to store the iCloud backups, or any apps, music or books you have purchased in the Apple ecosystem.

History of Multiple Apple IDs

It is recommended that you have only one Apple ID per iPhone but there was a time when Apple required a different Apple ID for iCloud and for iTunes. Note that the newer iOS16 doesn't support multiple versions.

Sign in with Your Apple ID

- If you did not log in during configuration, do the following:

- Go to **Settings**.

- Tap **Sign in to your iPhone**.

- Enter your Apple ID and password.

- If you do not have an Apple ID, you can create one.

- To protect your account with 2-factor authentication, enter the six-digit verification code.

If you forget your Apple ID or password, see Recovering Your Apple ID.

A free iCloud account is part of your Apple ID. iCloud provides a free email account and 5GB of storage for emails, documents, photos and videos, and backups. Purchased music, apps, TV shows, and books are not included in the available storage. You can update your iCloud storage directly from the iPhone.

Note: Some iCloud features have minimum system requirements. The availability of iCloud and its services varies by country and region.

Use Your Apple ID

You can use the Apple ID Number to authenticate any App at this stage.

For instance, if you are running the new Apple ID Wallet App, you can choose an Apple ID Number from that list and select the app to which you want to use that Apple ID.

You will then be prompted to authenticate the Apple ID.

You are then using the iMessage and FaceTime apps. You will need to use the Apple ID Number to get in touch with your Contacts and use the built-in Voiceover feature to hear the information.

You can see that you only need to use your Apple ID to sign in, but it is also used when opening the App Store.

View Your Apple ID Account Info

You can view your contact details, registered devices, security, and iCloud payment setup.

1. Go to **Settings** and tap on your **Apple ID banner**.

APPLE ID   31

2. Scroll down and select a device you want to view or remove from your account.

    ○ If you want to remove a device, scroll to the bottom and tap on **Remove Items**.

3. Most of the iCloud details are at the top of the **Apple ID** page. Tap the details you want to change. You can change your name, phone number, email address, birthday, password, registered phone number.

4. Tap on "Payment & Shipping" to change your credit card number, expiration date, and shipping address.

Add a Photo

You can also add a photo to your Apple ID.

  • Open **Settings** > **[Your Name at the top]** (underneath will be Apple ID, iCloud, Meida & Purchases)

  • At the top of the **Apple ID** page, will be a half circle with your initials with **EDIT** underneath – tap the **EDIT** link.

  • You'll be prompted to **Take Photo**, **Choose Photo**, **Browse** or **Cancel**.

Reset the Apple ID Number

Someone often uses Apple ID Numbers as their unique Apple ID. If you change your Apple ID, for example, you will want to change the number to no longer use your old Apple ID Number.

    This is because an Apple ID Number is linked to the phone. So if you change your number, you can use a different Apple ID for your App.

    You can use the iCloud.com web page to reset your Apple ID number. To do this, you need to go to your iCloud.com page and use the Apple ID Number you saved.

Change Your Apple ID Settings

There may be times that you want to change your information. Apple makes it pretty easy.

    Go to **Settings**> **[your name]**.

Do one of the following:

1. Update your contact information.

2. Change your password.

3. Manage Family Sharing.

SETUP EMAIL

Create an Email Account

Move to **Settings** > **Mail** > **Accounts** > **Add Account** to add an account.

Take one of the following actions:

- Select an email provider from the drop-down menu—for example, iCloud or Microsoft Exchange—and then input your email account credentials.

- Touch **Other**, then **Add Mail Account** to create a new account.

View Email

- Open the **Mail** App

- You will see a list of all the <**Email Addresses**> under **Mailboxes**

- Click on any of your <**Email Addresses**> to look at details or view the emails received at that Email Address.

  - Inside the email address, there is a circle with 3 lines on the left side of the bottom menu. Click this to see only the unread emails.

How to Modify the IP Address of the iCloud Private Relay

Private Relay routes web traffic to an Apple-managed server that strips the IP address. After Apple removes the IP address, the traffic is routed to a different server maintained by a 3rd-party company. That gives a temporary IP address and then routes the traffic to its destination, halting your IP address, location, and browsing activity from being used to create a profile about you.

Once iCloud Private Relay is enabled, you can pick how the allocated IP address conceals your actual location. Suppose you still wish to get local information when surfing in Safari. In that case, the IP address can use your general location without being precise, which is the default option, or if you want a more private relay, the IP address can just add your country and time zone.

Whichever option you choose, here is how to configure it in iOS 15.

- Open Settings.

- At the upper part of the main settings menu, press your name.

- Select iCloud.

- Private Relay should be tapped.

- Select the IP Address Location option.

- Choose Maintain Global Location (the default setting) or Use Time Zone and Country.

- Switch on/off iCloud Private Relay

- On your iOS device, open the Settings app.

- At the upper part of the main settings menu, press your name.

- Select iCloud.

- Private Relay should be tapped.

- Toggle the switch next to iCloud Private Relay on/off. Confirm by pressing Turn Off Private Relay if you're turning it off.

How to Use Hide My Email to Generate an Email Address

The following instructions demonstrate how to use Hide My Email to establish a new dummy email address in Safari and Mail. Ascertain that your iOS gadget is running iOS 15 or a later version.

- Open **Settings** > **[Your Name/Apple ID]** > **iCloud**

- Select **Hide My Email** from the **Apps Using iCloud** section

- Press **Create a New Address**.

- Hit **Continue**, then provide an identifying label for your address. Additionally, you can make a note about it.

- Hit Next, then press **Done**.

- Emails can now be sent with a random email address in Mail or when asked to input your email address on a website in Safari.

How to Use Hide My Email to Deactivate an Address

Suppose you are not presently using a random email address created by Hide My Messages. In that case, you can deactivate it temporarily to prevent receiving forwarded emails from it.

- Open **Settings** > **[Your Name/Apple ID]** > **iCloud**

- Select **Hide My Email** from the **Apps Using iCloud** section

- Select the email address to deactivate from the list.

- Select the Deactivate email address option.

- Press **Deactivate** to confirm.

How to Change Your Keyboard

On iPhone, you can change the default Keyboard by going to General, selecting Keyboard, and selecting a new Keyboard layout. However, there will be only a single Keyboard layout like English on your iPhone. Still, you can change the Keyboard's language to any other language.

- To change the keyboard of the iPhone, you need to open the Settings app and go to General. Here, you will see an option called Keyboard. When you click it, you will be directed.

- Here you will see all the keyboards available on your iPhone. The keyboard will be displayed accordingly

- when you select English or any other language.

- To change the keyboard's language, open the Settings app and select General. Here, you will find a setting called "Keyboard" and the available languages under it.

- Select the language you wish to use for the keyboard on your iPhone and click the keyboard to change the layout.

- When the keyboard changes to your selection, you can use it.

Note: If you want to change the keyboard layout for your iPhone without any cost or additional configuration, go to the settings app and click General, select Keyboard, then click a new keyboard layout.

APPLE MUSIC

How to Listen to Music

- From the **Home** screen, click on the **Music** icon: This will open up the Library view. When you open the Music App for the first time, you may see a screen telling you to sign up for Apple Music. You can ignore and dismiss this for now.

- Select the **Library** item at the bottom.

- **Choose from any of these options:** Playlists, Artists, Albums, Songs, Genres, Compilations, and Downloaded Music. You will also see Recently Added.

- Tap on **Songs**. Here you will see all the tracks.

How to Subscribe to Apple Music

- Go to iTunes or the Apple **Music** app or go to music.apple.com to subscribe.

- Go to **Listen Now** or For You and tap the **Trial Offer**.

- Choose a subscription (individual, family, or student). You can share your family subscription with 6 people.

- Sign in with your Apple ID or create a new one if you don't have one.

- Confirm your billing details and add a payment method.

- Tap or click **Join**.

Use Headphone Volume Features

Additionally, you can use the **Settings** app to set the maximum decibel level that keeps the headphone sound comfortable.

Reduce Headphone Loudness in Settings

- Go to **Settings** > **Sounds & Haptics** > **Headphone Safety**

- Turn on **Reduce Loud Sounds**, then drag the slider to the desired level

Improve Audio Measurement Accuracy of External Bluetooth Headphones

- Classify your Bluetooth device as a headset, speaker, or another device.

- Go to **Settings** > **Bluetooth**, then tap the **Info** button (i with circle around it) next to the device name.

- Tap the **Device Type**, then pick a rating.

Check the Headphone's Level While Listening

- Go to **Settings** > **Control Center**, then click the + sign next to **Hearing**.

- Plugin your headphones, then turn on the sound.

- Open **Control Center**, then tap the **Hearing** button (looks like ear)

iCloud

How to Set Up iCloud

iCloud is a service that allows users to easily store and sync data on multiple devices, and it works with all kinds of gadgets. Here are the features you get when you set up iCloud:

- **Cloud Storage:** Store any data in a safe and accessible place online. The more you add, the more you can keep.

- **Send an update to all your devices:** This allows you to share changes to any device you're using.

- **Remotely view your devices:** If you're away from home, you can pull up your files remotely from any web browser and on your phone.

- **Manage all your devices in one place:** You can access all your devices on the iCloud website or through your iCloud app, as well as your Apple TV.

Setting up iCloud on your iPhone is as simple as running the iCloud Setup Assistant on your iPhone.

- Open the **Settings** > **[Your Name]** > **iCloud**

- Enable the Apps and settings you want to backup.

You can also use iTunes to import your settings:

- Follow the on-screen instructions when your iPhone restarts and asks you to set up your iCloud account.

- Once complete, you will again be presented with the setup assistant - enter your Apple ID and password, then select Sign In.

BOOKS & MEDIA

The following sections describe the contents of the Lower Menu Bar of the Books app.

Read Now

- Select **Read Now** to access the books and audiobooks you are presently reading.

- Scroll lower to view the books and audiobooks you've included in your archive and the books you've checked out. Also, you can set day-to-day reading targets and keep track of the books you finish throughout the year.

Library

- Select **Library** to see every book, audiobook, sequence, and PDF via the Book Store or manually included in your archive.

- You can click **Collections** to see your books sorted into collections, such as **Want to Read**, **My Samples**, **Audiobooks**, and **Finished**.

Bookstore

- Select **Bookstore** from the bottom menu to see what books are available for purchase.

- Checkout the **Top Charts** and **New & Trending** sections

Audiobooks

- Select **Audiobooks** from the bottom menu to peruse the selection of audiobooks.

- Similar to the **Bookstore** – Checkout the **Top Charts** and **New & Trending** sections

Search

- To find a specific title or author, use. the Search button of the Lower Menu Bar.

How to Read a Newspaper or a Book

- Launch **Books**, then select **Book Store** or **Audiobooks** to surf for headings or hit on **Search** to find an exact title, author, or genre.

- Hit on the book's cover to view additional info, read an illustration, listen to a preview, or mark what you intend to read.

- Tap on **Buy** to acquire a title or tap on **GET** to download an available title.

- All purchases are made using the payment method associated with your Apple ID.

Reading books

- **Page turn:** Tap on the right side of the page or swipe right to left

- **Return to the previous page:** Tap on the left side of the page or swipe from left to right.

- **Move to an exact page:** Hit on the page and drag the slider at the lower part of the display left or right. Or select the find knob, enter the page number, and then hit the page number in the Find box.

- **Close the book:** to show the controls, click in the middle of the page, then click the Back button.

Bookmark a Page

- To add a bookmark, press the **Bookmarks** icon.

- Tap the **Bookmark** again to delete it.

- To see all your bookmarks, tap the **Table of Contents** button, then select **Bookmarks**.

Highlighting or Underlining a Text

- Press and grip a word.

- Slide the grab point to modify the chosen.

- Hit on **Highlight**.

- Tap the color picker button to choose or underline the shading color.

- Adding comments.

- Touch and hold a word.

- Move the grab point to adjust the selection.

- Tap a note, use the keyboard to enter text, then tap Done.

Sharing Selection

- Touch and hold a word, then

- Move the grab point to adjust the selection.

- Tap **Share**, then chooses a method.

Accessing Your Books on All Devices

- Move to **Settings** > **[Your Name]** > **iCloud**.

- Then, switch on both **iCloud** Drive and **Books**.

Syncing Reading, Library, and Archive

- Move to **Settings** > **[Your Name]** > **iCloud** and switch on both **iCloud** and **Books**.

- Then move to **Settings** > **Books** and switch on **Reading Now** and **iCloud Drive** in the **Syncing** section

Changing Day-To-Day Reading Goal

- Open the **Books** app

- Tap **Read Now** in the lower Menu Bar

- Then, scroll down to **Reading Goal**.

- Tap **Read Today**, then tap **Set Goal.**

- Move the counter up or down to set the minutes you want to read per day, then tap Done.

Changing Yearly Reading Goal

- Open the **Books** app

- Tap **Read Now** in the lower Menu Bar

- Then, scroll down to **Reading Goal**.

- Tap the placeholder box or book cover, then tap **Adjust Goal.**

- To set the number of books you want to read annually, move the counter up or down, then tap **Done**.

- Click the **X** in the top right corner to close the **Books Read This Year** page.

Organizing Books in the Books App Section

Creating a group and adding books to it. You can create your collections to customize your Library.

- Tap **Library**, tap **Collections**, and then tap **New Collection**.

- Name the group, for example, Beach Readings or Book Club, and tap Done.

Adding books to a collection

- Tap the **More** info button under the book cover (or on the book details page in the Book Store), tap **Add to Collection**, and select **Collections**.

- You can add the same book to multiple groups.

Arranging Books in Your Library

Choose how books are arranged and displayed in your Library.
- Tap **Library**, then scroll down and tap the word that appears next to **Sort** or Sort by.

- Select **Recent**, **Title**, **Author**, or **Manual**.

- If you choose manually, click and grip the book cover.

- Then, drag it to the position you want.

Reading PDF Docs in Books Apps

Right in the **Books** application, you can launch and save PDFs obtained in Mail, Messages, and any application.

Launch PDF Files in Books
- Tap a PDF add-on to launch it.

- Tap the Share button, then tap Books.

Sharing and Printing PDF Documents
- Open the PDF document.

- Tap the Share button.

- Then, choose a sharing option like AirDrop, Mail, Messages, or Print.

Highlight PDF

- Open the PDF and

- Press the **Markup** button to use the drawing tools and annotations (click in the middle of the page if you don't see the Markup button).

Viewing PDF Files on All Devices

- Switch on **Books**.

- Move to **Setup** > **Books** and toggle on **iCloud Drive**.

- Toggle on and set up Pro Max.

- Touch and hold the side key or the Sleep/Wake key (based on your mobile type), pending when the Apple badge displays.

- Hit on Set up by hand, then trail the pop-up setting up directives.

- Whenever you have another iPhone, iPad, or iPod touch running iOS 11, iPadOS 13, or later, you can automatically use Quick Start to fix up your newest gadget. Keep the 2 devices closer together, then trail the pop-up directives to firmly copy the various setup, favorites, and settings to iCloud Keychain.

MAKING CALLS & SENDING TEXTS

Set Up a Contact Account

- Go over to **Settings** > **Contacts** > **Accounts**.

- Select Add Account.

- Tap Other.

- If your organization supports CardDAV, select Add LDAP Account or Add CardDAV Account, and then enter your server and account information.

Contact

The **Contact** app is where you can manage and view your contacts list. **Add**, **Remove**, and **Modify**.

- To add a new contact, go to the **Contacts** app and click on the plus sign +. Siri also offers suggestions for new connections based on your usage of apps such as **Mail** and **Calendar**. To turn off this feature, **Settings** > **Contacts** > **Siri & Search** > Turn off 'Show Siri Suggestions for Contacts.'

- To find a specific contact, click the **Search** field in **Contacts** and input a name or phone number. A match will give you the Contact you are looking for.

- To share a **Contact** with someone on your Contacts list, locate the contact in your Contacts list and click **Share Contact**. A list of share options will be presented to you.

- To delete a contact, locate the contact in your list, click on the **Contact**, **Edit**, and then **Delete Contact.**

How to Add a Contact and Organize/Lock Them

The steps include:

- Touch the Contacts app icon from your device's home screen, which looks like an address book with greyed-out man and woman forms. You can also launch the Phone app with a green symbol and a white phone and then touch the Contacts icon on the bottom toolbar.

- Tap the Plus button in the top right-hand corner of your screen to add a new contact.

- Type the contact's first and last name and other pertinent information, such as their phone number, email address, postal address, birthdate, website URL, etc. You must fill out at least one of these areas to save the contact. You can also upload a photo by clicking the "Add photo" icon at the top-left.

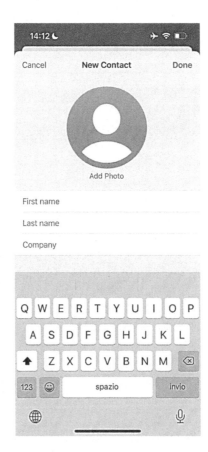

- To save the contact, click "Done" in the top right-hand corner of the screen after you're done.

iMessage

The iMessage App is a built-in messaging app that comes with every iPhone. It is available for all iPhone users and allows you to communicate with friends using iMessage. In addition, Apple allows users to send messages, images, videos, and stickers on iPhones. The iMessage App also allows users to send files and location information. It even has some features unique to the iOS device, such as the 'Send' button on the lock screen (for quick access).

How to Send Messages Through iMessage App

If you have enabled a contact on your Apple device, it will display on the contact book, and you can click on the person and select iMessage (IM). In addition, you can chat via the iMessage app and share photos.

When you send messages via the iMessage App, there are some special features like as:

- When you receive a voice message, it will show like a missed call.

- You can easily share a contact from the contact book.

- You can share photos and make a video call.

- Sharing of text, messages, and URLs through the iMessage App.

Setting up with the Help of the iMessage App

- Make sure the iMessage App on your iPhone is turned on. Let's navigate to Settings -> Messages and iMessage and check the setting of the iMessage App.

- Once you have enabled the iMessage App on the iPhone, you are all set to use the iMessage App.

Using iMessage App

- Browse and Download iMessage Apps

- In the Messages chat, hit on open the iMessage App Store.

- Click on an app to see more details and reviews, tap Price to purchase the app, or tap Get to download the free app.

- All purchases are made via the payment process related to your Apple ID.

- In a chat, hit on the iMessage application in the application drawer.

- Select an item in the iMessage application to include it in the message bubble.

- Include a note if required. Then hit on to send or terminate your message.

How to Send a Text Message to Add Contacts

The steps:

- Launch the text message from the person whose contact information you want to add.

- At the top of the screen, tap their phone number.

- Tap the "info" option in the menu immediately below the phone number.

- Touch the arrow to the right of the field showing the phone number on the Details page that appears.

Note: This will bring up an empty contact screen.

- Select "Create New Contact" and enter the person's first and last name.

- To complete adding the contact, tap "Done."

How to Import Contacts from Your Recent Call Records

Import contacts through the following ways:

- Tap the Recents symbol on the bottom toolbar of the Phone app, which has a green icon with a white phone on it.

- Tap the details option to the right of the phone number you wish to add as a contact under the Recents page.

- Tap "Add New Contact" on the blank contact screen that opens.

- Please enter the contact's name as you'd want it to appear on your phone and any other pertinent information, such as the contact's website URL, email address, etc.

- To complete adding the contact, click "Done."

How to Block and Unblock a Number

Here's how to unblock a number that you previously banned on your iPhone so that the contact may call, text, or FaceTime you again:

- Select a phone from the Settings menu. Touch Settings > FaceTime on your device that does not have the Phone app.

- Select Blocked Contacts from the drop-down menu.

- Swipe right to the left across the number in the Blocked Contacts list, then press Unblock.

How to Unblock Text Messages

If you banned somebody in Messages to prevent them from texting you, you could unblock their number in the Messages settings, and they will be able to contact you again.

- Go to Settings and choose Messages from the drop-down menu.

- Scroll down to Blocked Contacts and press it.

- After swiping right to left on the number you wish to unblock, tap Unblock.

- Unblocking Callers from Your Contacts List

- Unblock the banned number from their Contacts listing if it belongs to someone in your Contacts list. Find the person's entry in the Contacts app. It should be tagged.

- Then hit Unblock this Caller at the foot of the person's contact information.

Customize Text Message Tones

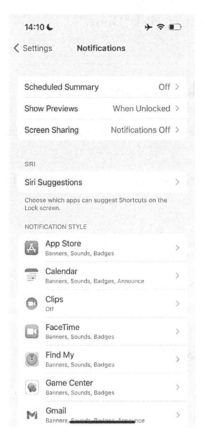

Apple has continued to push messages forward over the last few big OS releases, and iOS 15 is no different, with a massive pile of new features. The messages app has got an impressive overhaul to enhance your texting experience. There is much to discover, from emoji search to revamped emoji and new options within group chats.

Pinned Conversations

Pinned conversations go right to the top of your messages, making them easy to track. As usual, swipe to the left to Mute or Delete a conversation. To use this feature:

- Swipe from left to right on a conversation you want to pin.

- Tap the Pin icon.

- When you receive a message in a pinned conversation, it will appear at the top, and you can tap it to open it. You can pin up to 9 conversations that sync across the messages app on your iPhone, iPad, and Mac.

To unpin a chat:

- Tap and hold the pinned conversation

- Select the Unpin option.

Spice Up Your Messages with Special Effects

If you're trying to send a text after you're done typing the message, use a 3D-touch on the send button (which is a hard press on the message). a 3D-touch will bring up many effects you can add to the message, like slam, gentle, invisible ink, etc. These added features make messaging more fun and exciting. You can also experiment to see what works for you best.

Group Chats

You can now change the name and photo of a group conversation by tapping "Change Name and Photo" at the top of the group conversation. Before iOS 14, you could add a group name, but in this new interface, you can add a group name, photo, or emoji.

At the top of the conversation, you'll see all the group members, with the most recently active ones showing up as a larger icon.

To start a new conversation:

- Tap the "pen" icon at the top right of the messages screen.

- Type in the name of the people you want to start a group chat with.

- Type your message in the text field, and tap send.

To add an icon to the group chat:

- Open the group conversation.

- Tap on the Group icon at the top.

- Tap the small "info" icon.

- Tap "Change Name and Photo."

- You can set a photo, memoji, or emoji as the group icon.

- After you select a photo, tap Done.

Inline Replies

The messages app in iOS 14 allows you to reply directly to a specific message within a group chat as an inline reply. To do this:

- Hold down on a particular message within the group chat.

- Tap reply.

- Type your reply and send it.

- It will appear as a thread rather than another message in the conversation.

- To view a particular message thread, tap on it to expand.

Mentions

You can tag people within a group conversation.

- Type a name in the message input field.

- Tap on the little bubble suggestion that will pop up.

- Type your message and send.

The person mentioned in the text is notified that he was discussed, even if they muted the conversation.

How to Make Video Calls

Use Siri. Just speak "dial" or "call" and then follow it with the phone number of the person you want to call. Try to pronounce each number in the phone digit separately for a fast and prompt response.

If you don't want to use Siri, you can send a number using the following methods;

Click on Keypad [at the bottom right of the Call window]

Carry out any of the actions below:

- **Use a different line:** On your iPhone 13, click on the line at the top to select a line if you have more than one SIM (iPhone 13 is a Dual SIM).

- **Enter the number using the keypad:** Just tap on the

back arrow if there is any mistake while filling in the number that you want to call on the keypad.

- **Redial the last number:** Click on the

to see the last phone number you called or dialed, and then click on the

- **Paste a number you have copied:** Tap on the phone number field above the keypad for about 3 seconds (make sure you don't lift your finger for 3 seconds) and then select Paste.

- **Enter a soft (2-second) pause:** Touch and hold the star (*) key until a comma appears.

- **Enter a hard pause (if you want to pause dialing until you click the Dial button):** Touch and hold the (#) key until a semicolon appears.

- **Enter a "+" for international calls:** Place your finger on the "0" key until you see the "+" sign.

- **Tap on the**

to send the call:
You can also terminate the call by tapping on the

Call Your Favorites

Click on Favorites, and then select one favorite to call. Since iPhone 13 is a dual SIM device, it is capable of selecting lines for your call in the following ways:

- If you have set a preferred line for your calls, the iPhone 13 will use that line to send the call.

- The iPhone 13 can also use the line you used to receive the last call from the Contact or the line you used to send the last call to the Contact.

- The default line for voice.

You can manage your Favorites list by doing any of these:
- Add a favorite: Click on the

, and then select a contact.
- Rearrange or delete favorites: Select Edit.

Redial or Return a Recent Call

- Use Siri. You can say something like: "Hey Siri Redial the number I called last" or "Return the last call."

- You can as well carry out any of the actions below.

- Tap on Recents, and then select one number to send a call.

- To access more details about a particular call and the call sender, simply click on

- A red badge will normally indicate the number of missed calls.

Call Anyone on Your List of Contact

- Use Siri. Request Siri to send a call for you. Say something like: "Hey Siri, Call David's mobile."

Or do any of the following:
- In your Phone app, select "Contacts."

- Tap on the contact, and then click on the phone number that you want to send a call to. The call will usually be sent with the default voice line if you have not set any preferred line for that particular contact you want to call.

How to Send Emergency Calls

When an emergency comes up, you can use your iPhone to call for help. With the Emergency SOS, you can now easily call for help and send notifications to your contacts on the emergency list.

If you share your Medical ID, your medical information can be sent by your device to the emergency services when you text or call 911 (the United States only).

- From the Lock screen, tap Emergency.

- Input the emergency number (for instance, 911 in the United States.), and then tap

- Use Emergency SOS (all countries or regions except India)

- On your iPhone 13, press and then hold the side button together with the volume up or volume down button. When you see the Emergency SOS, do not lift your hands from the buttons until you get a warning sound and a countdown begins (the countdown can be skipped by dragging the Emergency SOS slider). Once the countdown stops, your iPhone will send a call to the emergency services.

- Or, you can even allow your iPhone to initiate Emergency SOS anytime you click your side button 5 times. To do this, navigate to the Settings app

, click on "Emergency SOS," and then enable [turn ON] the "Call with Side Button."

- Once the emergency call has been sent successfully to the emergency contact you had earlier selected, your iPhone 13 will notify the emergency contacts about your active location if it is available.

How to Answer or Decline Incoming Calls

If you are busy, you can silence incoming calls. However, you can still answer or decline a call depending on whether you are busy or not. By declining a call, the call goes to voicemail.

Answer a call

Carry out any of the actions below to answer your call:

- Click on

- You can also drag the slider in case your device is locked.

Silence a call

- Click on the side button to silence your call. Once you silence a call, your device will no longer ring out loud, and you can focus on what you are doing.

- You can also use either the volume up button or the volume down button to silence your call.

- You can still attend to a call you silence before it goes to voicemail.

Decline a Call and Send It Directly to Voicemail
- You can use any of the methods described below to decline a call on your iPhone and forward it to voicemail.

- Quickly press the side button twice.

- Click

- you can also decline a call by swiping up on the call banner.

Swipe down on the call banner to have access to more call options.

How to Insert a SIM Card

Insert the SIM card in the box of the iPhone. Make sure the sim card is fully inserted.
- Open "Settings" on your iPhone.

- Go to "General" > "About."

- Scroll down to "Hardware" > "SIM Status."

- If the SIM card is present in the phone's body, "Inserted" is selected in the text "SIM Status."

Using Stickers

If you downloaded a sticker application from the play store, you can improve your picture and videos with labels in messages.

- In a chat, hit on Apply stickers in the app drawer.

- Press and grip a sticker, then move it to the upper part of the message in the chat. Before launching it, you can do the resulting below:

- **Adjust angle:** Drag the sticker and move the other finger around the finger.

- **Adjust size:** Drag the sticker to move the other finger closer or farther away.

- You can also apply the sticker to another sticker or a photo.

- Double-click the sticker to see the text covered on the sticker.

- Select and grip a sticker, then hit on Sticker Details to see more information about a sticker. Next, you can do the ensuing:

  - Verify who sent the poster.

  - Find the iMessage app that sent the stickers.

  - Remove Label—slide left, then click Delete.

  - Manage iMessage applications.

  - Tap in the app drawer.

  - Tap Edit, then try out one of the subsequent with your iMessage app:

    - ***Reorder applications:*** Drag.

    - ***Include an application to favorites:*** Tap.

    - ***Get rid of an application from your preference:*** Tap.

    - ***Hide the apps:*** Exit the apps.

    - ***Erase apps:*** Slide left on the apps, then hit on erase.

FACETIME

Facetime (Features and Usage)

FaceTime is the easiest way to video call your friends and family on an iPhone. FaceTime works in the same way on all iPhone models. To start a FaceTime call, open the FaceTime app and tap the New FaceTime icon in the top-right corner of the screen.

Next, tap the phone number of the person you wish to talk with. Then, you must tap the Call option to make a FaceTime call.

To make a FaceTime call on iPhone XS and iPhone XS Max, tap on the camera option and then tap on the desired mode of FaceTime.

After you tap on the camera, select the mode you want to use. For example, you can choose between Face-to-Face mode, Video Calls, and Audio Calls and make the call.

How Does Facetime Work?

You can switch to different 'conversations' with different contacts in the FaceTime app.

In each conversation, you can:

- Send voice or text messages.

- Make video calls.

- Share photos.

- You can also make FaceTime calls to a single contact or a group of contacts.

FaceTime calls are encrypted using Apple's iMessage standard and can be made using the FaceTime app.

Choosing Who You Want to Video Call

- When you first open the FaceTime app on your iOS device, you'll see a list of people you've been in contact with over the past year.

- Your Contacts, people you call or message regularly, will appear in the list.

- Tap the name of someone you want to call, and a box will appear with the person's details.

- Tap the green camera button to start making a video call, tap the red 'end' button to stop making a video call, or tap the white 'not now' button to dismiss the call box and move on to other things.

- To add someone to your Favorites list, tap the menu button on your device (the one in the top right-hand corner of the FaceTime app) and tap Favorites. Then, tap the person's name to add them to the Favorites list.

- If you've been in contact with someone, they'll also be listed in your Contacts, so you can tap their name to add them to the list.

Facetime Requires an Internet Connection

To make a FaceTime call, you need an Internet connection.

You can change the Wi-Fi settings on your iOS device or move to a Wi-Fi hotspot to make sure you can connect.

How to Make Video Calls

Step 1. Open the FaceTime app

- You'll see your contacts list when you open the FaceTime app for the first time.

- Tap on the name of the person you want to call, then tap the green camera button.

Step 2. Share a photo with your caller

- Your FaceTime caller can share a photo with you, or you can take a picture yourself and send it.

- **To share a photo:**

  ○ Tap on the photo button at the bottom of the video call window and then tap the photo button that appears.

○ The camera will appear on your device's screen and capture the image.

- **To take a photo:**

  ○ Tap on the photo button at the bottom of the video call window and then tap the camera button that appears.

  ○ To cancel a photo, tap on the photo button at the bottom of the video call window and tap Cancel Photo.

  ○ To return to FaceTime, tap the photo button at the bottom of the video call window and tap Video Call.

Step 3. Share your location

You can share your location with FaceTime callers.

- You can open the 'sharing' window in the FaceTime app when you're both on the same Wi-Fi network.

- Tap on the 'sharing' button that appears, and tap 'start location sharing.'

- Your location will be shared with your FaceTime callers in the 'sharing' window.

- To cancel your location share, tap the 'sharing' button, tap on the menu button, tap Stop Location Sharing, and then tap Done.

- To turn location sharing off, tap the 'sharing' button that appears and then tap off.

Step 4. Chat privately

You can also chat privately on a FaceTime call.

- If you both have the private chat feature turned on in the FaceTime app, you'll see a small box to the right of the green camera button in the video call window.

- Tap to turn the feature on or off.

- You can also switch to private chat in the FaceTime app.

- Tap the Menu button, tap Private Chat, and then tap the Private Chat button that appears.

How to Receive a Facetime Video Call

- Tap on the green camera button at the top of the video call window, and then tap on the name of the person calling you.

How to End a Facetime Video Call

- To end a FaceTime call, tap the 'End' button at the top of the video call window.

- You can also end a FaceTime call from your Mac or Apple Watch.

- Tap on the red 'end' button at the top of the video call window, and then tap on the name of the person calling you.

Set up iPhone FaceTime

Go to FaceTime Settings, then toggle FaceTime on.

Do any of these:

- Set up your FaceTime calling account: Click Use Your FaceTime Apple ID, then click Sign In. Note: You can create one if you do not have an Apple ID.

- **Incalls, highlight the speaker**: Turn speech on.

- **In FaceTime chats, take live photos:** Turn FaceTime Live Photos on.

Activate FaceTime Call

- Ask Siri. "Make a FaceTime call."

- Tap New FaceTime at the top of the screen in FaceTime.

- In the input area above, type the name or number that you wish to call. Then, click the FaceTime icon to make a video call or the Audio call button (not available in all countries or regions).

- You may also hit the Contact Add button to open contacts and add persons or tap a suggested call history contact to make a quick call.

Tip: Rotate iPhone to use landscape orientation to view more during a FaceTime video chat.

Receive a FaceTime Call

Tap any of the following when a FaceTime call comes in:

- Take the call: Drag the tap Accept or drag the slider.

- Remove call: Press Decline.

- **Set a callback reminder**: Press Remind Me.

- **Send your caller an SMS message**: Tap Message.

The screen for the incoming call. The Remember Me and Message buttons are at the bottom of the screen, in the top row, from left to right. The Decline and Accept buttons are on the bottom row from left to right.

Rather than accept, you see the End and Accept option, which ends the previous call and links you to the incoming call when another call comes in.

Tip: You can have Siri advised to accept or refuse incoming calls by your voice.

Start a FaceTime conversation call from Messages

You can initiate a Facetime call in a message conversation with the person with whom you are chatting.

At the top right corner of the Message chat press the FaceTime button.

Do any of these:

- Tap Audio FaceTime.

- Tap Video FaceTime.

Send a Message

Do one of the following if no one answers your FaceTime call:

- Click leave Message.

- Click Cancel.

- Tap call back.

Call Again

Tap the name or number of the individual(s) you wish to call again in your call history.

FaceTime Sound Settings

The FaceTime app's spatial audio sounds like you have friends in your room. However, their voices are dispersed and sound like they come from every individual's direction on the screen.

   Note: Space audio is available on supported models only.

Filter Sounds from the Background

You can turn on Voice Isolation mode if you want your voice heard clearly in FaceTime and extraneous sounds filtered out (available on supported models). Voice isolation priority in FaceTime better your voice and blocks environmental noise.

- Open Control Center, press Mic Mode, and select Voice Isolation during FaceTime.

Enable All Sounds During Facetime

You can turn on Wide Spectrum Mode if you want your voice and all sounds in a FaceTime call (available on supported models).

- Open the Control Center, touch Mic Mode, and choose Wide Spectrum during a FaceTime call.

Switch the Sound Off

- Hit the screen for FaceTime (if not shown), and then tap the MuteOff button to turn off the sound. Next, make a selection of the FaceTime controls.

- Tap the button again to reactivate the sound.

   If your sound is turned off, your mic will detect if you talk and notify you that your microphone is silent and that you can hit the On button to enable it.

View FaceTime Participants in a Grid Structure

You can observe participants in tiles of the same size grouped in a grid during a chat with 4 or more persons in the FaceTime app. The tile of the speaker is immediately highlighted, so who speaks is easy to know. (Some tiles may seem fuzzy depending on your model.)

- Tap the Grid button in the lower-left corner of the screen in a FaceTime call (if you can't see the button, tap the screen).

- Tap it again to turn the grid off.

Create a Link to FaceTime call

With the iPhone FaceTime app, you can link a FaceTime call and send a link (through mail or messages) to a friend or group, which can be used to join or initiate a call.

- Select an option to send the URL (Mail, Messages, and so on).

How to Make a FaceTime Call

- Ask Siri: "Make a FaceTime call," you may say.

- Tap New FaceTime towards the top of the screen in FaceTime.

- After entering the name or number, you want to call in the top box, tap the FaceTime button to make a video call or the Call button to initiate an audio call (not available in all countries or regions).

- You may also hit the Add Contact icon to open Contacts and add people from there or tap a suggested Contact from your Call History to call them immediately.

Tip: Rotate your iPhone to landscape mode for a better view during a FaceTime video chat.
When a FaceTime call comes in, select one of the options below:

- Accept the following phone number: Accept by dragging the slider or tapping it.

- Tap Decline to end the call.

- Set a callback reminder by tapping Remind Me.

- Tap Message to send a text message to the caller.

- The Remind Me and Message buttons are located at the bottom of the screen, in the top row, from left to right. The Decline and Accept buttons are on the bottom row, from left to right.

- When a FaceTime call comes in while you're on another call, instead of accepting it, you'll see the Stop and Accept option, which will end the previous connection and connect you to the incoming call.

Tip: Siri can broadcast incoming calls, so you may accept or refuse them with your voice.

Start a Facetime Call from a Messages Conversation

In a Messages conversation, you may start a FaceTime call with the person you're talking to.

At the upper right of the Messages chat, tap the FaceTime button.

One or more of the following suggestions may be helpful:

- From the menu, choose FaceTime Audio.

- Select FaceTime Video from the menu.

Leave a Message

If your FaceTime call goes unanswered, try one of the following options:

- Tap the Leave a Message button.

- Press the Cancel button.

Call Back

- In your call history, tap the name or number of the person (or group) you want to call again.

- Remove a phone number from your list of contacts.

- In FaceTime, swipe left over the call in your call history, then hit Delete.

Create a Link to a Facetime Call

You may generate a link to a FaceTime call in the iPhone's FaceTime app and send it to a friend or a group (through Mail or Messages), so they can join or start a call.

- Tap Create Link close to the screen top.

- Select a method for sending the link (Mail, Messages, and so on).

- You may plan a remote video meeting in the Calendar by selecting FaceTime as the meeting venue.

Note: Anyone may join you on a FaceTime call, even if they don't own an Apple device. They may participate in one-on-one, and group FaceTime calls right from their browser, with no need to log in. (They'll need the most recent version of Chrome or Edge.) H.264 video encoding is required for video transmission.)

Take Live Photo

To take a FaceTime Live Photo, go to **Settings** > **FaceTime** and turn on **FaceTime Live Photos**, then perform one of the following:
- Use the Take Picture button when you're on a call with someone else.

- On a Group FaceTime conversation, press the tile of the person you wish to picture, then hit Full Screen, then Take Picture.

Use Other App During Facetime Call

While using the FaceTime app to make a call, you may use other apps to look for information.
- Go to the Home Screen and tap an app icon to open it.

- To return to the FaceTime screen, tap the green bar (or the FaceTime icon) at the top of the screen.

Make a Group Facetime Call

In the FaceTime app, a group FaceTime chat may include up to 32 participants (unavailable in all countries or regions).
- Start a FaceTime conversation with a group of people. Tap New FaceTime towards the top of the screen in the FaceTime app.

- Type the names or phone numbers of the people you want to call in the top field.

- You may also access Contacts and add contacts by tapping the Add Contact icon. Alternatively, you can tap suggested contacts from your phone history.

- To make a FaceTime visual call, press the FaceTime button; to make a FaceTime audio call, tap the Call button.

- Swipe through the row to discover a participant you don't see. (If a picture isn't available, the participant's initials may show on the tile.)

- Go to Settings > FaceTime, then switch off Speaking under Automatic Prominence to avoid the person speaking or singing tile growing bigger during a Group FaceTime chat.

- Note that sign language detection necessitates the use of a supported presenter model.

Backup and Sharing

Automatically Update iPhone

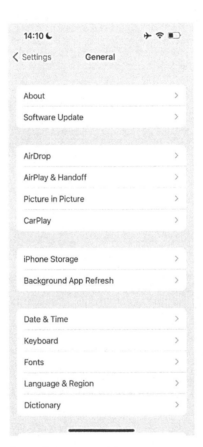

When you first set up your iPhone, if you did not enable automatic updates, perform the following:

- Enter **Settings** > **General** > **Software Update** and select **Automatic Updates**.

- Turn on **Download iOS Updates**, and **Install iOS Updates**.

- If an update is available, iPhone will download and install the update overnight during charging and Wi-Fi connection. Before an update is installed, you will get a notification.

Manually Updating iPhone

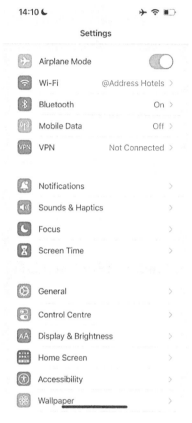

You can always check for software updates and install them.

- Enter **Settings** > **General** > **About** > **iOS Version**.

    ○ The screen shows whether an update is available and the currently installed version of iOS.

- Click **Settings** > **General** > **Software Update** > **Automatic Updates** to switch off automatic updates.

Back up with iCloud

- Enter **Settings** > [your name] > **iCloud**

- Toggle the **iCloud Backup** switch to ON (green).

- When the iPhone is powered, locked, and connected to Wi-Fi, iCloud automatically backs up your iPhone daily.

Note: Your carrier can provide you the possibility to back up your iPhone using a cellular network on models supporting 5G.

- Tap Back Up Now to initiate a manual backup.

- Go to **Settings** > [your name] > **iCloud** > **Manage Account Storage** > **Backups**. Choose a backup and tap **Delete Backup** to remove a backup from the list.

Note: When you enable an iCloud feature (like iCloud photos and contacts) under **Settings** > [your name] > **iCloud**, its data will be stored in iCloud. All of your information is automatically up to date on all gadgets, as a result of the iCloud backup.

Back-Up with Mac

- Connect your cable to your iPhone and your PC.

- Choose your iPhone from the **Finder** sidebar (left side of Finder under **Locations**) on your Mac.

- MacOS 10.15 or later is needed to utilize the Finder to back up the iPhone. Use iTunes to back up the iPhone with previous versions of macOS.

- Click **General** on the top of the Finder window.

- Pick "Back up all iPhone data to Mac."

- Pick "Encrypt local backup" for backup data encryption and protection using a password.

- Press the **Back Up Now** button.

Note: If you're running Wi-Fi, you can wirelessly connect your iPhone to your computer.

Restore iPhone via iCloud backup

- Switch on a new iPhone or a recently erased iPhone.

- Follow the instructions for selecting a language and location online.

- Press **Manual Set Up**.

- Follow the instructions on-screen by tapping on **iCloud Backup Restore**.

Restore iPhone via PC backup

- Link a PC with your backup to a newly erased iPhone via USB.

Do one of these:
- In your Mac's Finder sidebar: Click **Trust** after selecting your iPhone.

MacOS 10.15 or later is necessary to use the Finder to recover the iPhone from the backup. Use iTunes to restore from a backup with previous versions of macOS.

- With an iTunes application on a Windows PC, click the icon at the top-left side of the iTunes window to select the newly deleted iPhone from the list if you have multiple devices linked to your PC.

- Click the "**Restore iPhone**" button on the welcome screen, choose your backup from this list, and click Continue.

- If your backup is encrypted, somebody must type in the password to restore the files and settings.

How to Backup iPhone

You need a Wi-Fi connection for this.

Back up Apps

1. Go to **Settings** and tap your Apple ID at the top. If prompted, sign in with your Apple ID.

2. Tap on **iCloud** and tap the switch next to the desired apps. Tap on the **iCloud Backup** app at the bottom of the list.

3. Turn on **iCloud Backup** and tap on **Back Up**. Wait for the backup to complete.

Back up Contacts

1. Go to **Settings** and tap on your Apple ID. Sign in if prompted.

2. Tap on **iCloud** and then switch on the **Contacts** switch. Select Merge contacts with iCloud if you are asked to.

3. Tap on the **iCloud Backup** app at the bottom. Turn on iCloud Backup and tap on Back Up.

4. Wait for the backup to complete.

Back up Media and Pictures from Phone

1. Go to **Settings** and tap on your Apple ID. Sign in if prompted.

2. Tap on **iCloud** and then tap **Photos**. Turn the iCloud Photo Library switch on.

3. Tap on **iCloud** to return to the previous screen. Next, tap the i**Cloud Backup** app.

4. Turn on iCloud Backup and tap on Back Up.

5. Wait for the backup to complete.

How to restore iPhone 13 to Default

A master reset restores your phone's default settings and may delete files on your internal storage.

- Back up all your data on the internal memory.

- If you enabled Apple FMiP Activation Lock, you need to access the internet to complete these steps.

- Head to **Settings**, then to **General**, and then select **Reset**.

Select from any of the options:

- Reset All Settings: Use this option before you attempt a master reset.

- Erase All Content and Settings: Use this option for master reset. Make sure you select Erase all and keep plans.

- Reset Network Settings: This will erase any saved Wi-Fi profiles.

- Reset Keyboard Dictionary

- Reset Home Screen Layout

- Reset Location and Privacy

- Enter your password if you are asked to.

- Confirm your selection.

How to Restore All Contents from Backup

Option 1:

Erase all current data. You can restore all your data if you backed them up via iTunes. if you do a restore with iTunes, all your current data will be erased. Use the following steps:

1. On your computer, open iTunes. Connect your phone to the computer and enter your passcode if you are asked to or select "Trust this Computer."

2. Select the device in iTunes or the Finder window to continue.

3. Click on "Select Backup" and then depending on the date, select the most relevant backup.

4. Click on "Restore."

Option 2:

Do not need to erase data (Recommend). If you don't want to remove all your current data, use PanFone Data Transfer to restore it.

1. Download and install PanFone on your computer. Launch the app.

2. Connect your device to the computer via a USB cable.

3. Click on the iTunes Backup File. Select "Restore" and click on "iTunes backup." If you have already synced your device with iTunes on the computer, then PanFone Data Transfer can detect the iTunes backup files. Click on "Next" to load iTunes backup from your computer.

4. Next, all saved iTunes backups will be enlisted. Select one backup according to its date or size. Then click Start.

5. Click on the Desired Contents from iTunes Backup. All data from the backup file will be available to restore. Just mark the ones you need then click "Next" to load the files. This might take a while depending on the size

6. Retrieve the Files from iTunes Backup to your device. Once the data is loaded, select the files you want to retrieve then click "Recover to Computer" or "Recover to iOS 14 device" as needed. After the process is complete, your device will automatically reboot. Do not disconnect the device until the process is successful.

Send Items with Airdrop

- Open the item and then tap on the Share icon or another button showing the sharing choices for the app.

- In the share choices row, press the **AirDrop** icon and tap on the AirDrop profile image of a user.

Tip: Position yourself close to another iPhone and click the user's profile image at the top of the screen.

- If the person does not display as an AirDrop user, invite them to open the iPhone, iPad, or iPod touches **Control Center** and enable AirDrop to receive items. To send to someone on a Mac, ask them to make themselves discoverable with Airdrop in the **Finder**.

Allow other people to transfer items via AirDrop to your iPhone

- Tap the **AirDrop** icon, open the **Control Center,** and touch and hold the top-left controls group.

- To select who you want to receive items from, tap **Contacts Only** or **Everyone**.

- Each request might be accepted or refused as it arrives.

How to Sync Personal Data

Synchronize Your Phone Data on iCloud.com

This will be the most obvious way to sync your phone data. If you use a personal iPhone, you probably want to back your data to iCloud because you use Apple services. You will probably do the same if you use iOS on your Mac.

You can find some of your data on iCloud, like SMS text messages, contacts, photos, videos, music, reminders, notes, voice memos, and more. If you were using iCloud before iOS 11, you probably can get your data back.

Synchronize Your Phone Data on Google

The Google cloud storage provides a way to sync your data in the cloud. People can do this by choosing to have their data on the cloud. There are better options than this if you use Google services. If you've used a Google device like a laptop or Chromebook, all your data will be synced from the cloud. You can use Google Drive or Gmail; Google Assistant will sync your data.

You could sync your data if you were using Google Drive or Gmail before iOS 11. If you have not used these services, I recommend Google Drive because Google Assistant will sync your data. You can sync your phone data, apps, browser bookmarks, contacts, photos, videos, emails, documents, and much more.

Synchronize Your Phone Data With OneDrive

OneDrive has been my go-to cloud storage service. This includes storing data, music, photos, videos, and documents. OneDrive offers 1 TB of cloud storage for free with unlimited access to your files. If you were using OneDrive before iOS 11, you could sync your phone data to the cloud.

If you're looking for something more extensive, you can store 5 TB of cloud storage with unlimited access to your files. You can share with other users or even sync your data.

Synchronize Your Phone Data With Dropbox

Dropbox has a cloud service that allows you to back up your files. All you need to do is set up Dropbox and use it to back up your files to the cloud. This will give you a place to back up your important files. You can store 5 GB of data and back up to 2 GB of photos, videos, and files with unlimited access to your files.

One of the best parts about Dropbox is how easy it is to set up. On your iOS device, go to the App Store and download Dropbox for free. Open it up and sign in to your Dropbox account, and that's it. It will sync all of your files.

SAFARI & THE INTERNET

Safari

Safari has a new look in iOS 15. Controls are relocated to the bottom of the screen, making them simpler to grasp with one hand.

A new, compact tab bar floats at the bottom of the screen, allowing users to slide between tabs effortlessly, and it also includes a Smart Search box. Tab Groups allow users to keep their tabs in a folder and sync them across iPhone, iPad, and Mac devices. The presence of a new tab overview grid view.

How to Disable Safari's Website Tinting

Tinting occurs when the Safari color interface changes to match the color format of the website you're viewing in the tabs, bookmarks, and navigation button sections.

Tinting allows the browser interface to fade into the background, creating a more immersive experience. However, the effect is not popular, and some people are turned off by it. Fortunately, Apple included a toggle switch to turn it off.

- On your iPhone, open the Settings app.

- Scroll to the lower part and hit Safari.

- Turn off the option next to Allow Website Tinting in the "Tabs" section.

Move Safari's Address Search Field to Top Section

- On the address bar's left side, press the "aA" symbol.

- In the pop-up menu, choose Show Top Address Bar.

Additionally, you can manage this design change under Safari's "Tabs" section of Settings -> Safari. Select Single Tab to move the URL bar to the top.

Download and Install Web Extensions for Safari

- Open Settings.

- Scroll to the lower part and hit Safari.

- Select Extensions from the "General" menu.

- Select more Extensions.

This last step will lead you to an App Store area devoted to Safari extensions, where you can explore and, if desired, download and install them. Please keep in mind that although some extensions are free, some contain features that need in-app payments to activate.

Once an extension is installed, it will appear in the Settings' "Extensions" section, where you can manage any extension-related settings.

Quickly Refresh Safari Web Page

Apple has retained the refresh symbol in the address bar, which you can touch to reload the currently viewed website. However, another less apparent method of refreshing websites you can find more conveniently exists. In Safari, refreshing a website is a downward swipe on any page. This alternative to pressing the reload symbol is particularly helpful if you want to keep the address bar at the top of the screen, where tapping the reload icon is inconvenient.

How to Customize the Start Page and Background of Safari

The Start Page has many configurable elements, such as customizing the Start Page background. Additionally, you can sync the look of your Start Page across all of your devices through iCloud. The following instructions demonstrate how to customize the Safari Start Page.

- Open Safari on your iPhone or iPad.

- Press the open tabs symbol in the Safari screen's lower right corner.

- To start a new tab in the Tabs view, touch the Plus symbol in the lower-left corner.

- At the bottom of the Start Page, scroll down and touch the Edit button.

- Turn on the option next to Use Start Page on All Devices to sync your Start Page settings with additional devices associated with the same Apple ID.

- Utilize the controls to customize what appears on your Start Page. Favorites, Reading List, Privacy Report, Siri Suggestions, Frequently Visited, Shared with You, and iCloud Tabs are all available choices. Also, you can enable the Background picture option and choose one of the pre-installed iOS wallpapers or create your own by pressing the large Plus icon.

- When finished, press the X in the top-right corner of the menu card.

Delete Tabs Group

When a Tab Group is no longer required, it is simple to remove it.

- Press the Open Tabs button in the lower right corner of the screen when reading a website.

- Touch the tab bar in the center at the lower part of the screen.

- In the upper left corner of the menu card, touch Edit.

- To delete a Tab Group, touch the circular ellipsis symbol next to it, then touch Delete.

All of your Tab Groups are synced across all of your gadgets, as in your iPhones and iPads running iOS and iPadOS 15 and Macs running macOS Monterey.

How to Make Your IP Address Untraceable

- With iPhone or iPad, choose the **Settings** app.

- Scroll to the bottom and select **Safari**.

- Scroll down to the "**Privacy and Security**" section and choose **Hide IP address**.

- **Trackers and Websites** or **Trackers Only** are the options.

How to Make a Private 'Hide My Email' Address

- With iPhone or iPad, choose **Settings** > **Your Apple ID Name** > **iCloud** > **Hide My Email**

- Tap the **Create new address** button.

- Continue, then give your address a unique label. You may also make a note of it if you like.

- Then, touch Next, and finally, tap Done.

HOME SCREEN

Create Folders

- Touch and hold the background of the home screen until applications start rattling.

- Drag an app to another app to create a folder.

- Into the directory, drag other programs. Multiple app pages can be included in the folder.

- Tap, hold the folder, click Rename, and enter a new name to rename.

- Tap the home screen background and try again if the apps start to jitter.

- Tap Done, tap Home Screen Background twice again when you've completed.

- If you want to delete a folder, click the folder to open it and shift all apps away. The folder is erased automatically.

Note: The Home Screen organization of your apps does not alter the app library structure.

- Send an application to the home screen from a folder

- You can transfer an app from the folder into the home screen to make locating and opening easier.

- Go to the home screen of the application folder and press the folder to open it.

- Touch the app and hold it till the applications start jiggling.

- Drag the app to the Home Screen from the folder.

Apple Pay

Apple Pay might be more accessible and safer than a physical card. You can make secure payments via Apple Pay at shops, in transit, in apps, and on websites supporting Apple Pay with your cards stored in the wallet application. Use Apple Pay to send and receive money from friends and families in messages and purchases from participating companies.

- Add debit, credit, and prepaid cards to your Wallet to set up Apple Pay.

- In the top half, several credit and debit cards will be shown at the Add button's top right-hand corner. (Provided solely in the US).

- Fill in your credit or debit card.

- Tap the Add Card button on Wallet. You may be asked to sign in using your Apple ID.

Choose one of these:

- Previous cards: Select the card you have paired with the Apple ID, the cards you use with Apple Pay or the deleted cards. Tap Continue and enter each card's CVV number.

- Credit card or debit: Put the iPhone in the frame, or enter the card details manually.

- Transit card: Enter the location's name or card or scroll down to see your area's transit cards.

Podcasts

Use the Podcasts app for science, news, politics, comedy, etc. You can follow it to add a show to your library if you locate a show you want. Then you can listen offline effortlessly, receive new episodes notified, and more. The search screen shows Top Charts, Comedy, Company, and Culture categories.

Note: Shows can offer paid memberships that allow you to access exclusive shows and episodes, fresh releases, ad-free episodes, etc. See Subscribe to an iPhone show or channel for managing your subscriptions.

Find Podcasts

- Title, person, or subject search: Tap Search at the bottom right of the screen and enter the search box on the top of the screen for what you are looking for.

- To see new shows: To view fresh and Noteworthy, featured movies and Apple-published collections, tap Browse at the bottom of the screen. To view the Top charts and explore by category, press Search.

- ○ Tip: Personalized suggestions are presented on the Listen-Now screen to assist you in discovering your next show when you listen to episodes.

- Add shows via URL: Press Library, click More and select Add Show with URL.

Note: Only enter URLs in the RSS format.

See Shared Podcasts

- You may find episodes a friend shared with you in Messages using the Podcasts app. (you must turn on Podcasts In Settings > Messages > Shared with your buddy, and your buddy should be in your contact.)

- Tap Listen Now and navigate the Shared Podcasts area to see Shared Podcasts.

See Episodes in a Particular Podcast

- Click a podcast to view the information page.

- Tap See All or scroll for recent episodes (if available).

DISCOVERING APPS

App Store Settings

- Select **Settings** > **App Store**

  - Setup Language

  - Setup whether Cellular Data should be used to download and install Apps

Discovering Apps in the App Store

Select **App Store** from the Home Page

Hit any of the following to discover applications, games, and in-app events:

- **Today**: highlighted articles, applications, and in-app events.

- **Games**: Browse dozens of categories to find your next game, including action, adventure, racing, and puzzles.

- **Apps**: Browse new releases, check out the top rankings, or search by category.

- **Arcade**: Enjoy selected premium games from Apple Arcade (membership needed) without advertising or in-app purchases.

- Enter your search term and then press **Search** on the keyboard.

- **Inquire of Siri:** You can make a statement such as "Search the App Store for educational applications" or "Get the Fifa app."

Purchase and Download an Application

- Scroll through the available apps.

- If there is a cost to download, the button will have a Price ($9.99). If the app is free to install the button will say **GET**.

- If you see a Redownload icon (Cloud with a down arrow) rather than a price, you have already bought the software and may re-download it for free.

- You may be asked to verify your Apple ID using your Face ID, Touch ID, or your passcode to complete your transaction.

Share an App

- Click on the App's icon to see additional information about the app.

- Select a sharing choice or hit Gift App by ping the Share icon (not available for all apps).

Redeem Apple Gift Cards

Click the **My Account** button or your **Profile Image** at the upper right.
   Select from the following:

- **Redeem a Gift Card or Code.**

- **Send a Gift Card through Email.**

Subscribe Apple Arcade

- Touch **Arcade** on the App Store and hit the subscription button.

- Examine the free trial period (if any) and subscription information, then follow the on-screen instructions.

Cancel Subscriptions for Apple Arcade

- If you cancel your membership, you cannot play any Apple Arcade games on your device, even if you have downloaded them. Delete any applications that you no longer need.

- You may resubscribe to Apple Arcade games and reclaim your gaming data. However, if you wait too long, you risk losing access to part of your gaming data when you resubscribe.

Switch Open Apps

Open the **App Switcher** to switch between apps on your iPhone fast. Then, you can start right where you left off when you switch back.

Open apps icons are displayed at the top, and the current screen for each app is shown underneath their symbol.

Work With App Switcher

In the App Switcher, do one of the following to display all open apps:
- iPhone with Face ID: Swipe from the bottom of the screen and stop at the middle of the screen.

- iPhone with a Home Button: Click the home button twice.

- Swipe right and press the app you wish to use in other to browse the open applications.

Switch Open Apps

Swipe right or left along the bottom of the screen to rapidly switch between open apps on an iPhone with a Face ID.

Customize Access for Particular Apps

For some apps, home screens, and settings, you can choose alternative display and motion settings.

Change the application settings
- Press Add app, then choose the app, Home Screen, or Settings.

- To change the settings, tap the app or Home Screen.

- Set the size of the text when using an application

- Tap the Text Size button after opening Control Center.

- (If the button Text Size is not visible, add it to the Control Center—go to Settings > Control Center and select Text Size).

- Shift the slider up and down to increase or decrease the size of the text.

- Tap All Apps at the bottom of the screen to alter the font size for all apps.

Maps

How to Search for a Place on Maps

Find Places in Maps

You may search for addresses, points of reference, services, etc., with the Maps app.

Looking for a Spot

- Ask Siri. Ask Siri. "Show me the Golden Gate Bridge".

- Alternatively, tap the search field (at the top of the search chart).

- The search card shows "8th and market" searches and various results. Search results.

In several ways, you can search. For instance:
- Crossroads ("8th and Market")

- Area ("Village of Greenwich")

- Landmark ("Guggenheim")

- Postal code ("60622")

- Business ("films," "San Francisco CA Restaurants," "NYC Apple Inc")

Get Driving Instructions

Step 1: Do One of These

- Say, "Hey Siri, give me the direction to the mall."

- Hit your target location (like search results in Maps or a landmark) or click and hold anywhere on the map, then tap the directions button.

Step 2: You Can Do Any of the Following When a Suggested Path Appears

- Shift to the driving direction: If you don't have driving as your default mode of traveling or if you are looking at a transit map, press the Drive button to see a proposed driving path.

- Select a future departure or arrival time: Tap Leaving Now, select a day or time for departure/arrival (at the top of the route card), then tap Done. Due to the forecast traffic, the estimated journey time can change.

- Avoid highways or tolls: scroll down to the base of the route card and set the selection.

- Pick additional route options: You can reverse the start and destination, pick a different start or destination, and more.

Step 3: Tap Go for the Path You Prefer
On the way, Maps speaks about your destination on a turn-by-turn basis.

Look for Your Parked Car

You get a parked car marker on Maps to get back to your car if you disconnect the iPhones from your car's Bluetooth or CarPlay system and exit the vehicle.

- To locate your vehicle, select Parked Car on the search card below Siri's suggestions.

- Go to Settings > Maps and switch off Show Parked Location to turn off the parking space.

Display or Conceal the Compass or Speed Limit

Enable or disable Compass or Speed Limit from Settings>Maps, then tap Driving under directions.

Get Walking Directions

Step 1: Do One of These

- Say, 'Hey Siri, give me walking direction home.'

- Hit your target location (like search results in Maps or a landmark) or click and hold anywhere on the map, then tap the directions button.

Step 2: You Can Do the Following When There Is a Suggested Route

- Switch to the walking path: If your default mode of travel is not walking or viewing a transit map, press the Walk button to display a suggested walking route.

- Choose additional route options: You can reverse the start point and destination, pick a different start or destination, and more.

Step 3: Tap Go for the Path You Prefer

Step 4: Tap on the Pedestrian AR button, then take the displayed instructions; tap Close to go back to the map.

Note: If you lift your iPhone after taping the Pedestrian AR button, instantly return to the augmented reality screen, go to Setup > Maps > Walk, then toggle on Raise to View.

Enable Location Services on Find My App

You must enable location services on your iPhone to use the Find My app. Then, the flows below will guide you.

- Launch the **Settings** app.

- Tap **Privacy**.

- Next, press **Location Services.**

- Toggle on **Location Services.**

- Suppose you'd like to share your location with others. In that case, you can do that from this Settings area by pressing Share My Location and turning on the toggle on the resulting interface.

Another way to do this is demonstrated below.

- Launch the **Settings** app.

- Touch your Apple ID at the top

- Press "Find My"

- Next, turn on Share My Location.

Locate Family/Friends on Find My App

If you need to locate someone who has shared their location with you, it's straightforward.

- Launch the "Find My" app.

- Touch People at the bottom and touch the person on your list. You'll then view their location on the map.

- You also have preferences to Contact them, get Directions to their spot, add Notifications, and many other things.

Share Your Location via Find My App

To share your location, launch Find My and tap "Me" at the bottom. Ensure the toggle is activated for Share My Location.

You can also elect to Allow Friend Requests, choose to Receive Location Updates with everyone or only people you share with, and Edit Location Names.

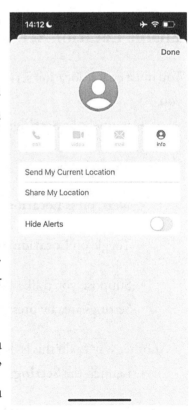

Enable Offline Finding via Find My App

- Launch the "Find My" app and press Devices at the bottom. You'll see all your devices on the list at the bottom, including their locations on the map.

- Tap to select a particular device and then Play Sound to assist you in finding it or get Directions to it. You can also "Mark As Lost" and get Notifications when the device is found. Finally, if you deem it fit, you can remotely Erase This Device.

You can also use this feature to find iOS devices belonging to others who've shared their location with you. For instance, if your friend lost their device, their devices will show up in the list for you to choose and locate the same way you locate yours.

Verify Offline Finding Is Active & Enabled

- Open the Settings application.

- Press your name up top to view your Apple ID settings.

- Press the "Find My" option.

- Next, press "Find My iPhone."

- Make sure "Enable Offline Finding" is turned on on the page that pops up.

Share Your Location

You have to configure location sharing before you can use the Find My app to share your location with friends.

Note: When setting up sharing locations and others still cannot see your location, be sure that Location Services is on in Settings > privacy > Location > Find My.

Create Location Sharing

- Tap Find My at the bottom of the screen in the Find My app and activate Share My Location. Under my location appears the gadget that shares your location.

- If your iPhone doesn't currently share your location, scroll down and click Use this iPhone as My Location.

Note: From the iPhone, iPad, and iPod touch, you can share your location. Click Find My on the gadget and adjust your location to that gadget to share your location from another device. When you share your location with an Apple Watch (GPS+Cellular Models) from an iPhone, your location will be shared on Apple Watch when your iPhone is out of range.

You can also adjust your location-sharing settings, Click settings, and select [Your name] > Find My.

Set Your Location Label

You can make a label more meaningful for your current location (like Home or Work). You will notice the label beside your location when you tap Me.

- At the bottom of the screen, hit the Location Name Edit button.

- Choose a label.

- Touch Add Custom Label, enter a name, and tap Done to add a new label.

Share Location with Friend

- Tap plus sign, then select Share My Location.

- Also, at the end of the screen, touch People, scroll down to the bottom of the people's list, and tap Share My Location.

- Type the name of a friend you wish to share within the field (or tap the Add Contact button and select a contact).

- Tap Send and select how long your location is to be shared.

Add iPhone to Find My

- Go to Settings > [your name] > click Find My on your iPhone. Please enter your Apple ID if you are requested to sign in. If you don't have one, then follow the instructions, tap "Don't have an Apple ID or forget it?"

- Tap Find My iPhone, then turn on Search My iPhone.

- Turn on one of these:

  - If your device is offline (no Wi-Fi or cellular), find "My" can locate your device using Find My network.

○ Send Last Location: If the charge level of your smartphone gets critically low, its Location Transfer to Apple.

To check your device on the map and play a sound there, you can utilize Find My on your iPhone. You see the position of the device when the gadget is online. If the system is offline, the last time the device was online or connected to Find my network, you can view the location of the device.

See the Device's Location

You can view its location on the Find My App if your device is online. Tap Devices at the base of the screen and tap the device name you want to find.

If it can be located, the gadget appears on the map to see where it is.

If the device cannot be located: under the device's name, you see "No location found." Turn on Notify when Found under Notifications. Once it is located, you will receive a notification.

Play Lost Sound on Other Devices

• Tap Devices at the end of the screen and tap the device name on which you prefer the sound to be played.

• Click Play Sound.

If you're using the device: After a brief while, a sound starts and progressively grows in volume, then plays for around 2 minutes. Then, the gadget vibrates (if applicable). A Find My [device] alert is displayed on the device screen. Your Apple ID email will also be sent an email to confirm.

You can see Sound Pending if the device's offline. The sound is played the next time the device is connected to a Wi-Fi or mobile network.

AirTag

AirTag can be registered with your iPhone to your Apple ID. When lost, you may use the Find My app to find your iPhone if you attach it to an everyday object such as a keychain or a backpack.

Add an AirTag

• Go to your iPhone's Home Screen.

- Remove the AirTag battery tab and hold it next to your iPhone. If relevant.

- On your iPhone's screen, tap Connect.

- Select a Name in the list or select Custom Name, then press Continue to create a name and select the emoji.

- Go to your Apple ID, continue registering the item, and touch Finish.

Find My app also allows you to register an AirTag. Take either of these:

- Type the Add AirTag button.

- Click Items at the lower part of the screen, press Add New Item, then tap Add AirTag at the bottom of the Item List.

- You need to delete it before adding it if this item is registered in someone else's Apple ID.

Change Airtag's Name or Emoji

- Tap items below the screen and tap the AirTag you wish to edit its name or the emoji.

- Tap Rename item.

- Select the name in your list or select Custom Name to write the name and choose Emoji.

- Tap done.

Remove an AirTag

- You can still delete it from your account if it isn't close to your device. However, before anyone may register it with their Apple ID, the item must be reset.

- Follow the on-screen guidelines and tap Remove item.

Get Walking Directions in Augmented Reality

In a nod to Google Maps, the new augmented reality mode uses your iPhone's back camera to overlay walking instructions onto the actual environment, making it simpler to see where you need to go in densely populated places and eliminating the need to glance down at your smartphone as you go.

Create a walking path first, then raise your iPhone and scan the surrounding buildings when asked. The step-by-step instructions will display automatically in AR mode, making navigating simpler, particularly when the directions are confusing. The augmented reality functionality will be accessible in key supported cities beginning in late 2021, including London, Los Angeles, New York, Philadelphia, San Diego, San Francisco, and Washington, DC.

How to Locate Transit Stations Near You

- Pull up the menu card in the Maps app and press More close to "Favorites."

- Select Nearby Public Transportation from the "Siri Suggestions" menu. To add it to your Favorites, press the Plus symbol next to it.

- You'll see a categorized list of nearby transportation options. Press one to learn more about it, including the stops the train or bus has made and will make, other future departures for this destination, and delay information.

- To easily locate a route, scroll down to the bottom of the stops display and press Line Pin under "Line Options." You can also return to the previous Nearby Public Transportation menu and slide right on a transit line/route to see the yellow Pin icon.

Note that pinned routes will always display at the upper part of the "Nearby Public Transport" option. You can just unpin a path by swiping right on it to reveal a yellow Unpin icon.

HEALTH

The Health app in iOS 15 now has a new sharing option that allows users to share their selected health data with family or carers. Descriptions, highlights, and the ability to pin findings for fast-access have been added to lab results. In addition, health can now detect Trends, alerting users to significant changes in personal health indicators.

Walking Steadiness is a new statistic added to the Health app to reduce fall risk. COVID using a QR code from a healthcare practitioner, 19 vaccinations and test results may be saved in the Health app. Blood glucose features entail interactive charts and illustrate values across sleep and activity.

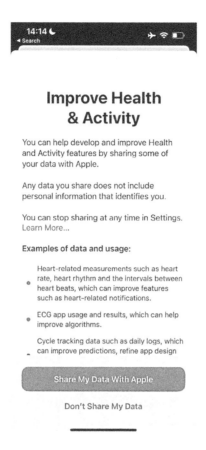

Add Health Data to iPhone Manually

Data such as measurements, symptoms, and menstrual cycle data can be entered manually in the **Health** App.

To view the screen for **Health Categories**, tap **Browse** at the bottom right and proceed as follows:

- Click a category (Scroll down to all Categories.)

- Click the search field and enter the name of a category or a specific data type (such as body measurements) (such as weight).

Do any of these:

Include info on the Cycle Tracking category.

- In the Sleep category, add information: Tap Add Data in the upper right-hand corner.

- To other Categories, add info: To edit the data, hit the Details icon and tap Add Data on the upper right.

Monitor Walking Steadiness

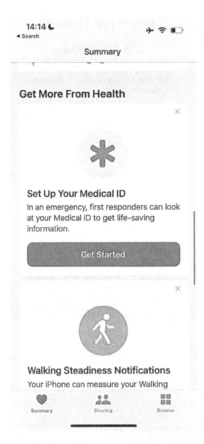

The health application employs special algorithms to analyze balance, strength, and gait when carrying your iPhone in the pocket or holder close to your waist. Suppose your steadiness becomes poor or remains low. In that case, you might receive a notification and share it immediately with someone near you. Health can also show you practice to increase the stability of your walking.

Get Notifications for Low or Very Poor Steadiness

- Open the **Health** app.

- Tap **Summary** at the bottom of the screen, then scroll down until you see the **Walking Steadiness Notifications → Setup** section.

- Tap **Setup** for walking stability notifications and then follow the directions in the display.

- Once enabled Walking Steadiness Notifications should appear on your Summary page.

See Your Data for Walking Steadiness

- Open the **Health** app. Tap **Browse** in the lower right, then tap **Mobility**.

- Click **Walking Steadiness** (you may need to scroll down).

- Click the Show Information button to learn about the 3 levels of steadiness (Low, Very Low, and OK).

See Health Trends

Once data have been collected over sufficient time, the health system can notify you of important changes in data categories such as heart rate rest, the number of steps, and the amount of sleep. Trend lines indicate how much and how long specific metrics have changed.

To see all the latest trends, tap **Summary** at the bottom left.

You can do the following if health has identified trends:

- See more trend data: tap graph.

- See further trends: Click see Health trends.

- The **Summary** screen shows trend data comprising sleep graphs, Blood Glucose graphs, and resting heart rate.

- From the **Summary** screen, select **Show All Health Trends**, tap "Manage notifications" to receive notifications about your health patterns, and then set Trends on.

View Highlights

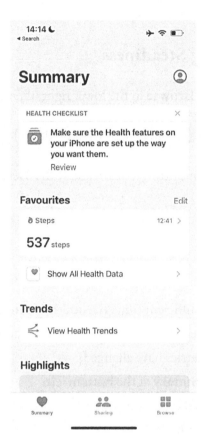

- To see your health and fitness highlights, click **Summary** at the bottom left.

- Tap the Details button to view additional details about a highlight.

A summary screen presents highlights, including minutes of exercise and sleeping blood glucose.

Check Headphone Levels Over Time

- Open the **Health** App, select **Browse** in the lower right toolbar, then select **Hearing**.

- Click Headphone volume, then do any of the ensuing:

  ○ **See exposure levels over time:** Hit on the tab at the upper section of the screen. (All levels are measured in volumes).

  ○ **Find out the volume rating:** Press the Show notification button.

  ○ **Modify the time shown in the graph:** Drag the graph left/right.

◦ **View information about a timeline:** Press and grip the graph, then slide to move the selection.

◦ **See information about typical exposure:** Hit on Show All Filters then hit on Daily Average.

◦ **See a line showing average exposure:** Hit Exposure at the lower section of the graph.

◦ **Show high and low ranges:** Display Show All Filters, then select a category.

◦ **Filter data via headsets:** Hit Show All Filters, slide to the lower part of the screen and choose a headphone.

◦ **See highlights:** Scroll down; to learn more, click Show All.

FUN WITH MEMOJI

Create Memoji

You can choose a custom Memoji, skin tone, hat, spectacles, and more. In addition, for different moods, you can create several Memoji.

The Memoji screen displays the character formed at the top and can be customized. The button Done is on the right top, and the button Cancel is on the left top.

- Tap the Memoji stickers button and click the New Memoji button during the chat.

- Tap every feature and select your preferences. By adding characteristics to your Memoji, your character comes alive.

- To add Memoji to your collection, tap Done.

- To modify, duplicate or delete a Memoji, click the Memoji Stickers button, press Memoji, and tap the More Options button.

Send Memoji Stickers

Sticker packs depending on your Memoji and Memoji characters are automatically generated. You may use stickers in unique ways to communicate several emotions.

- Tap the Memoji Stickers button during a conversation.

- To view the stickers in the sticker pack, tap the Memoji on the top row.

To send a sticker do this:

- To add a sticker to the message bubble, tap the sticker, add a comment if you like, then tap the Send button to send it.

- Touch a sticker, hold it, and drag it to the top of the comment. The sticker will be sent instantly when you add it to the message.

Memoji Recordings and Animated Memoji

You can send Memoji messages using your voice and reflect your facial emotions on compatible models.

- To check your message, tap Replay.

- To send a message, tap the Send button, or delete to cancel.

Making Memoji

In the chat, tap.

- Select every feature and pick the preference you require.

- Select Done to include the Memoji in your group.

- To edit, copy, or erase a Memoji, hit on the Memoji, then click.

- Send Memoji or Stickers

- In the chat, click.

- Hit on the Memoji in the upper row to see the labels in the sticker pack.

- Send a sticker. Check one following one:

  ○ Select a sticker to include it in the message bubble. Add a note if needed, then hit on to submit.

  ○ Toggle and grasp a sticker, then slide it to the upper section of the message in the chat. The sticker is automatically transferred once added to a Message.

AVOID DISRUPTIONS WITH FOCUS

Configure iPhone Focus

Concentration is a function that allows you to focus on a task by reducing distractions. Focus can temporarily stop any notifications or just enable certain notifications (for instance, those corresponding to your task)— and let other people and applications know that you are occupied.

You can select or build your Focus from the giving list.

Note: Open the Control Center, press Focus, then toggle on Do Not Disturb to silence all notifications swiftly. Do Not Disturb or Do Not Disturb when driving is included in Focus now.

Set Focus

You can set a given focus option, such as driving, personal, sleep, or work, or build an individual focus if you wish to focus on any specific activity. You can silence notifications or just allow people and applications notifications to fit your Focus—set up a Work Focus, for example, and only let your colleagues and work apps be enabled.

You can also customize a Home page with only related applications connected to your Focus, making this page the only one available during your Focus.

Five focus alternatives were shown on a screen—don't interfere, drive, work, personal, sleep. You may utilize the same Focus Settings on all your Apple devices with the same Apple ID on the Share Across devices button.

- Enter **Settings** > click **Focus**.

- For example, tap Focus—such as do not disturb, drive, work, sleep, or personal—then follow the instructions onscreen.

- You can always return to Settings > Focus and alter anything you want after setting your Focus (which is initially specified when creating your Focus):

- Choose (if any) people you prefer to get notifications from during Focus. Press People or Add Person, Select Contacts, and click Done.

- Choose if you wish to receive calls during this Focus: Tap Calls from then choose —Favorites Everyone, No One, and All Contacts. Allow repeated calls to be activated (two or more calls within 3 minutes by the same person).

- Finally, tap the Return button in the top right-hand corner.

  ○ Note: Calls from your emergency contacts can always be received regardless of your focus settings.

- **Select applications during Focus from which you want (if any) notifications**: Tap Apps or Add Apps, choose Apps, and tap Done.

- **Select if you wish to allow all apps during this Focus to get time-sensitive notifications immediately:** Switch on Time Sensitive and press Back at the upper left.

- Choose if you want apps to show quiet notifications: Tap Focus Status, then activate or deactivate Share Focus Status. When you activate it, people will see that you have silence notifications but not which Focus you have enabled.

- Select (if applicable) the home screen pages you want to visit in Focus: Click Home Screen, switch on a custom page, select a home page you want to utilize, and hit Done.

Tip: The applications for this Focus can be moved to one home screen page, and then pick that page.

Personal Focus Mode Setup

First, let's look at the Personal Focus Mode and how you can set up and customize it in the best possible way.

- **Step 1:** Slide down the control center on the iPhone from the top-right corner of the Home screen.

- **Step 2:** Long-press on the "Do Not Disturb" toggle on the controls menu to invoke the preview of the Focus modes.

- **Step 3:** Click on the 3-dot option (…) option at the left corner of the Personal Focus mode panel to redirect you to an info page about the mode.

- **Don't miss out:** This feature allows notifications from important contacts and apps and silences notifications from other platforms across all apps.

- **Share you're away:** This feature tells your contacts that you are away and cannot respond to any calls with a notification status that says you are silenced. So, if your loved ones are trying to get to you and may be worried about why you haven't responded yet, it clears them off with that notification. Tap the "Next" button highlighted in blue to proceed.

- **Step 4:** The following screen lets you add the list of people or contacts you want to receive notifications and calls from even when "Do Not Disturb" is active. The first icon menu in grid form has a button with an 'Add Person' tag beneath it, which redirects you to the list of contacts on the iPhone so you can pick the ones you wish to receive notifications from.

- **Step 5:** On the bottom of the screen are 2 options, which are "Allow" and "Allow none." These 2 options are designed to set up the list of apps you wish to receive notifications from while in the Personal Focus mode. By default, Personal Focus Mode may suggest certain apps on the iPhone on the list of apps you should allow alerts from, such as your regularly accessed apps. In addition, it has the same plus (+) button to redirect you to the iPhone's list of apps to choose from.

- **Step 6:** On the screen that displays apps on the "Allow" menu, tap the 'Allow' button at the bottom to take you to the next screen.

- **Step 7:** On the following screen with the caption "Your Focus is Ready" and other details about the mode, there is a "Done" blue bottom at the bottom. Tap on it to take you to the customization page of the Personal Focus Mode as you have successfully set it up.

Personal Focus Mode Customization

In the Personal Focus Mode screen is a list of options to customize the mode on the iPhone's Home screen layout, lock screen, and the scheduled date and time. You can also schedule the date and time for activation and deactivation of the Personal Focus Mode on the iPhone.

- **Home screen:** Inside the Home screen customization page are 2 options: "Hide Notification Badges" and "Custom Pages." The "Hide Notification Badges" toggle hides or mutes alerts on the iPhone's Home screen, even when the device is unlocked. The "Custom Pages" takes you to the different Home screen pages on your iPhone, so you can check off Home screens containing distractive apps to prevent them from displaying once the Personal Focus Mode is active.

- **Lock screen:** The Lock screen customization tab for Personal Focus Mode displays 2 toggles, just like the customization tab for the Home screen. The "Dim Lock Screen" and "Show on Lock Screen" toggles allow the customization of notifications. The "Dim Lock screen" toggle dims the lock screen immediately after the mode is activated. At the same time, the "Show on Lock Screen" shows the silenced alerts or notifications on the lock screen if toggled on.

- **Add schedule or automation:** Inside this option, you can do a lot with the schedule of the Personal Focus Mode, such as the time, location, and apps where it should be readily active on your iPhone. If you need more than just the "Time" schedule, you can tap "Time" amongst the list of options on the following screen. Here, you can set the start and end time for the Mode and check off the days you need the Personal Focus Mode to be active on the iPhone.

When you enable any Focus modes on the iPhone, they become active across all your Apple devices running the same iOS 15 software.

- You can add multiple Custom Focus Modes on your iPhone with the plus (+) icon on the extreme bottom of the Focus toggle menu when you long-press on it.

- Slide down and 3D-Press on the "Focus" icon from the top-right corner of the Home screen.

- The following screen shows you the list of modes under the Focus mode and a plus (+) button on the bottom of the display.

- Tap on the plus (+) icon, and the device will redirect you to a different list of other Focus modes, such as driving, fitness, gaming, reading, etc.

- Tap the "Custom" button with a plus sign (+), which appears as the first option on the list of addable Focus Modes.

- The following screen displays a type-box for naming the focus, color options, and icons to set up your Custom Focus Mode with a "Name Your Focus" tag above the screen.

- Tap on the type-box with highlighted "Name" text to name the new custom focus mode as you wish. You can also select the variant colors and icons to suit the Focus Mode you are setting up on your iPhone.

- After your Focus mode outlet is set up, tap on the "Next" blue button to proceed to the next step, where your iPhone will guide you to finish the setup.

- Aside from the default modes, you can add more from the list of modes onto the focus toggle on the Control Center menu.

How to Activate a Focus

It is simple to turn Focus on. Simply open the **Control Center,** press the **Focus** button, and choose the Focus you wish to enable. You may also activate it by tapping the ellipsis (3 dots) button, which will give options For **one Hour, Until Tonight**, **Until Tomorrow Morning,** or **Until I Leave this Place**.

How to Focus

- Goto **Settings** > **Focus**

- Tap the New Focus button (represented by a plus symbol) at the top right.

- To make a new Focus, choose Custom.

- Give your customized Focus a name and select a color/emoji/icon to make it stand out, then press Next.

- On the following page, tap Add Person to choose the individuals you wish to receive alerts while the Focus mode is active. You may also select to receive calls from Everyone, No One, Favorites, or All Contacts as a separate call-specific option.

- Allow [X] Person or Allow None to proceed.

- Tap Add App on the following page to select which applications you want to get alerts from when the Focus mode is active.

- Allow [X] Apps or Allow None to proceed.

- On the following page, select Allow Time-Sensitive Notifications while the Focus is activated or tap Not Now to make a later decision.

- To complete the custom Focus, tap Done.

How to Personalize a Focus

If you wish to customize a previously configured Focus, click **Settings** -> **Focus** and choose the Focus mode to change.

There are numerous settings accessible in the Focus choices. For example, you may modify the name and icon of the Focus by pressing it at the top of the menu, as well as the people and applications from whom you want to get notifications.

- Below is a toggle for turning Time-Sensitive Notifications on/off. People and applications can alert you instantly if you choose this option, even if you have the Focus switched on.

- Under "Options," you'll see Focus Status. Enabling this allows applications to notify those who contact you that your notifications have been Silenced. You'll also find the option to Conceal Notification Badges on app icons and the Custom Page toggle, which allows you to hide specific Home Screen pages. You may also opt to dim the Lock Screen's look and show any silent alerts you get on the Lock Screen.

- You'll see a Smart Activation option in the last section, "Turn on Automatically." When you enable this, the selected Focus will be activated automatically at relevant moments throughout the day, based on signals such as your location, app use, and more.

If this is too ambiguous, you may utilize the Add Schedule or Automation option to have the Focus switch on at a specific time automatically, location, or while using a particular app.

WEATHER

In iOS 15, the Weather app has been completely revamped. The Weather app now has more graphical weather data displays, a full-screen map, and a dynamic layout depending on outside circumstances.

Apple has updated the animated backdrops in the Weather app to represent the sun's current position and precipitation conditions appropriately. Also, additional alerts indicate when rain or snow begins and ends.

Check Weather Conditions

The weather screen shows the location on the top and the current climate and temperature, Rain. Below is a chart that shows a 10-minute increase in rainfall during the next hour. Below is the precipitation map and the hourly forecast. The Location List button is in the lower right corner, and the Show Map button is in the lower-left corner.

To do the following, open **Weather**:

- Check the local weather conditions: When you open the Weather app, you will get the details for your present location.

- The top of the screen shows updates on severe circumstances such as winter storms and flash floods. Tap to read the entire government warning (not available in all countries or regions).

- See hourly Forecast: Turn left or right on the hourly display.

- See the 10-day forecast: See the weather, precipitation, and high and low temperatures for upcoming days.

- Details on air quality: See information on air quality; tap See More for information on health and contaminants (not available in all countries or regions).

Note: When air quality reaches a given level, the air quality scale appears above the hourly forecast. The air quality scale is always above the hourly forecast in some regions.

- Look at your area's weather maps: View a map of the surrounding temperature, rainfall, or air quality. Tap on the map for a full-screen view or alter the map view for air quality, temperature, and precipitation.

- Further details More weather: Check the UV index, wind speed, sunrise, sunset, and more when you scroll down.

- In other places, check the weather: Wipe the screen to the left or right, or tap the icon for Edit Cities.

How to Read Full-Screen Air Quality, Precipitation, and Temperature Maps

Open the Weather app.

Turn on the weather map using the **Show Map** icon (lower left corner) to accomplish any of the following:

- To move the map, tap the screen and drag the finger.

- If you want to zoom in and out, pinch the screen.

- Zoom out to view the 12-hour precipitation provision while looking at the precipitation map; zoom back to see next-hour precipitation prediction (not available in all nations or regions).

- Tap the Favorite Locations icon to see a different place in your weather list.

- To return to your present location, tap the Current Location icon.

- Click and hold the place to add it to your weather list, see its current conditions or view it in Maps.

- The surrounding area is filled with a temperature map. The current and preferred locations buttons are in the upper right corner from top to bottom. In the center of the screen, you will find the following buttons on the menu to modify the display: Temperature, Air Quality, and Precipitation. The Done icon is in the upper left corner.

- To go back to Weather and Forecast, tap Done.

How to Make the Most of Apple's New Weather Maps

In Apple's native Weather app, 3 full-screen weather maps are offered. They provide a birds-eye perspective of local precipitation, air quality, and temperature forecasts. Unfortunately, air quality data is only available for Canada, China mainland, Germany, France, India, Italy, Mexico, the Netherlands, South Korea, Spain, the United Kingdom, and the United States.

Tap the little folded map symbol in the bottom-left corner of the Weather app, or scroll down on a forecast page, press on the default temperature map, and then tap on the stack to change the view to precipitation or air quality.

The precipitation maps are dynamic, displaying the direction of oncoming storms and the severity of rain and snow. The 12-hour forecast is shown in the progress bar at the bottom, which you may stop using the Pause button or scrub through by moving the progress dot with your finger.

The stack icon in the top right corner may be touched to transition to the air quality or temperature maps, showing you the conditions in your immediate vicinity and the neighboring locations. The icon above it allows you to move between geographical regions in your prediction list, while the top icon zooms in on your selected location.

Explore Weather Maps

Apple's standard **Weather** app got a significant redesign in iOS 15, partly due to the addition of many features from the famous weather app Dark Sky, which Apple bought in 2020. Among such features is weather maps, which this page defines and describes how to utilize.

Apple's native Weather app possesses 3 full-screen weather maps. They provide a bird's eye perspective of local precipitation, air quality, and temperature predictions. However, air quality data is only available for some countries like India, Italy, Mexico, Canada, mainland China, Germany, Spain, the United Kingdom, France, the Netherlands, South Korea, and the United States. The maps are accessed by clicking the small folded map symbol in the Weather app's lower-left edge or moving down a forecast screen, pressing the default temperature map, and then clicking on the stack to switch to precipitation or air quality.

The animated precipitation maps depict the path of approaching storms and the intensity of rain and snow. The progress bar at the bottom displays the 12-hour forecast, which you can stop using the Pause button or scroll through using your finger to move the progress dot. Touch the stacked symbol in the top right corner to transition to the air quality or temperature maps, which provide a visual representation of the conditions in your immediate region and the neighboring areas. The icon above allows you to navigate your forecast list's geographical regions, while the top icon zooms in on your selected location.

Note that you can zoom in or out on any map to better understand the selected weather data.

Checking the Weather on iPhone

Use the Weather app to check the prevailing weather for your current location and places you may travel to. On the Weather app, you can see upcoming hourly and 10-day forecasts, view harsh weather information, see weather maps, get notifications about precipitation, and lots more.

Note: The weather app uses your Location Services to obtain the forecast for your active location.

To activate the Location Services, navigate to Settings > Privacy > Location Services, choose Weather, and select an option. Activate Precise Location by turning it ON to increase/improve the accuracy and preciseness of the forecast in your active location.

Use Siri. You can say something like: "What is the weather for today?" or "How rainy is it right now in California?"

Follow the step below to check the weather forecast and conditions in your location or any other locations.

- Open the Weather app to perform any of the actions below.

- **Check local weather conditions:** When you open the Weather app, the details for your active location will be available.

    ○ Updates about harsh weather conditions like flash floods and winter storms appear at the top area of the screen. You can tap to read the full government-issued alert (this is not available in all regions or countries).

- **See the hourly forecast:** Simply swipe the hourly display to the left or right.

- **See the 10-day forecast:** Access weather conditions, the chance of rain, and information about high and low temperatures for the coming days.

- **View air quality details:** Access information about the quality of air. Tap See More for details about pollutants and health information (not available in all regions or countries).

Note: The air quality scale will appear just above the hourly forecast when air quality gets to a certain level for that particular location. The air quality scale usually appears just above the hourly forecast for some places.

- **View weather maps in your location:** See a map that tells you about temperature, air quality, or precipitation. Tap on the map to see it in full screen or switch the map's view between rainfall, temperature, and air quality.

- **Access more weather details:** Move down to see the UV index, sunset, sunrise, speed of the wind, and more.

Add, Delete, and Rearrange Locations in Your Weather List

- Tap to view your weather list.

- Carry out any of the actions below.

  - **Add a location:** Input the name of the city, the city's zip code, or the airport code inside the search field, select the location, and then click Add.

  - **Delete a location:** Swipe left on the location, then click. Or click and then click on "Edit List."

  - **Rearrange the order of locations on the list:** Touch and hold the location, and then move the location up or down. Or, click and then select "Edit List."

REMINDER LISTS

Creating, Editing, or Deleting Lists and Groups

You can categorize your business, school, or purchase reminders in lists and groupings. Do any of these:

- Creating a Fresh list: Click add list, select an account, input a name, then select a color and symbol for the list if you have more than one account.

- Create Group List: Tap Edit, Touch Add Group, enter a name, then tap Create. Or drag a list to a different list.

- Set up lists and groups: Touch, hold, and drag a list or group to a new place. You can even transfer a list to another group.

- Modify a list or group name and appearance: Go to the left list or group, then hit Edit Details.

- Delete a list or group, including reminders: Move, then tap the Delete button on the list or group.

Use Tags

Tags can organize your reminders quickly and flexibly. You can search for or filter reminders throughout your lists with one or more tags, such as #shopping and #work.

- Add tag: Type #, write a tag name, or pick a tag from the menu above the keyboard when creating or editing a reminder. A tag can only be one word, but it can be combined with dashes and underscores. You can add several tags to your reminder.

- See reminders using tags: Type a tag or All Tags in the Tag Browser (under your custom list). Then, tap more tags at the top of the list to filter the list further.

A screen that displays several lists of reminders and smart lists. The browser tag is in the lower part.

NOTIFICATIONS

View and Answer Notifications

Notices help to keep track of what is new—whether you missed a call or moved an event date or more, they let you know. The notification settings can be customized to only view what is important to you.

3 groups of notifications, 2 notification groups, 3 mail notifications, 2 slack notifications, and one calendar notification:

Search Notification

In the Notification Center, make one of the following to display your notifications:

- On the lock screen: Swipe up from the center of your screen.

- On other screens: Swipe down from the upper middle on other screens if there are previous notifications; you can scroll up to see them.

Swipe up with 1 finger from the lower screen or click the home button to close the Notification Centre (on an iPhone with a Home button).

Reply Notifications

If multi-notifications are available in the Notification Center or the lock screen, they are organized by an app that makes it easier to view and manage. Some app notifications, such as the theme or the thread, can also be divided by organizing features in the application. Groups appear as little stacks with the latest notification at the top.

Three notification groups and 1 notice on the lock screen: 2 notifications for messages, 3 notices for mail, 2 notifications from Slack, and 1 notification from the Calendar.

Do one of the following:

- To expand the notifications group to view individually: Tap the group. Click Close the Group, and click show less.

- **To view a notification and conduct fast actions (on compatible models) if offered by the app:** Touch the message and hold it.

- **To open a notification application**: Click the notification.

Plan Notifications Summary

You can schedule a summary of your notifications to be displayed daily at a particular time. This lets you reduce interruptions during the day and catch up quickly when convenient. Furthermore, based on how you use your apps and the most relevant notifications above, you may modify and personalize the notification's summary smartly according to priority. The summary is convenient when you utilize Focus to delay messages while concentrating on a task.

In the Notification Settings, a summary of the alerts that occurred since the planned summary was activated is stored in the Notification Center until the scheduled summary display time.

- Choose the apps to monitor in your summary.

- Set your summary time. Tap Add Summary if you want another summary.

- Click A–Z below Apps Summary, then ensure that the apps you wish to include are enabled in your summary.

- Display recent notifications on the Lock Screen.

- The **Notification Center** can be accessed on the Lock Screen.

- Enter **Settings**, move to **Face ID and Passcode** (for a Face ID iPhone such as the iPhone 13) or Touch ID and Passcode (for other iPhone models).

- Input passcode.

- Switch **Notification Center** on and move down (below **Allow Access When Locked**).

SIRI

Siri queries in iOS 15 are handled on-device utilizing the Neural Engine, enhancing security and considerably increasing responsiveness while eliminating the need for an internet connection.

As you use your smartphone, on-device speech recognition and understanding improve. Siri may also learn about the contacts you engage with frequently, new phrases you write, and subjects you read about to deliver more relevant replies.

Siri can now transmit images, web pages, material from Apple Music or Apple Podcasts, Apple News stories, Maps locations, and other onscreen things in a Message or even capture a screenshot to send. Furthermore, Siri may now utilize onscreen context to send a message or make a phone call.

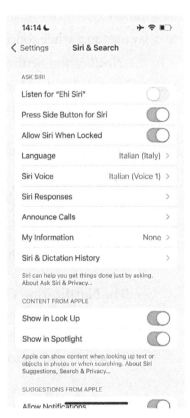

Siri is now better at retaining context between requests, allowing you to refer to what you previously requested in a discussion. You may also request to operate a HomeKit gadget at a particular time or under specific conditions, like when you leave the house.

On AirPods and in Apple CarPlay, Siri may also Announce Notifications like Reminders, and users can ask Siri what is on their screen.

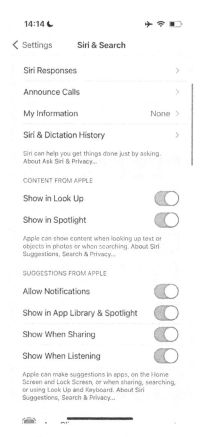

Siri can now deliver neural text-to-speech voice in Swedish, Danish, Norwegian, and Finnish languages. Siri also supports Mixed English, Indic, and a blend of Indian English and a native tongue, such as Hindi, Telugu, Kannada, Marathi, Tamil, Bengali, Gujarati, Malayalam, and Punjabi.

Siri and Dictation

How to Instruct Siri to Control Your HomeKit Devices at a Predetermined Time

For example, if you want your blinds to open at 7 a.m. the next day, you might tell Siri, "Hey Siri, open the blinds at 7 a.m." Siri also responds to geolocation instructions, so you can say things like, "Hey Siri, turn off the lights when I leave."

When you ask Siri to operate a HomeKit product this way, automation is created in the Home app's "Automation" section. If you wish to delete an Automation generated by Siri in the Home app, slide the Automation left and hit Delete.

In iOS 15, HomeKit developers may also add Siri functionality to their goods. However, it should be noted that using Siri commands with third-party devices requires owning a HomePod to pass the requests through.

Third-party HomeKit gadgets with Siri integration can be managed using Siri commands for tasks like scheduling reminders, controlling devices, broadcasting messages, and more.

How to Use Siri While Not Connected

You don't need to activate anything for Siri to operate offline once you've upgraded to iOS 15. The following are the sorts of queries that it can process without contacting Apple's servers:

- Timers and alarms can be set and deactivated.

- Start the applications.

- Control the audio playback of Apple Music and Podcasts.

- Control System Settings like accessibility features, volume, Low Power Mode, and Airplane mode, among others.

If you don't have a cellular data or Wi-Fi connection and ask Siri to do something that requires internet access—such as messaging someone, getting weather updates, or watching a video—you'll get a response like "To do that, you'll need to be online" or "I can help with that when you're connected to the internet."

How to Make Siri Read Your Notifications

In iOS 15, here's how you get Siri to announce alerts.

- Open the Settings app.

- Select Notifications.

- Choose Announce Notifications via the "Siri" menu.

- Toggle the switch next to Announce Notifications to the ON position in the green.

To have Siri broadcast all notifications from a single app, just choose it from the "Announce Notifications" list and enable the Announce Notifications option.

How to Use the Translate App's Auto-Translation

- To activate Auto Translate, first enter conversation mode by tapping the Conversation tab, which can be found at the bottom of the screen in both landscape and portrait mode.

- Bottom-right, tap the ellipsis (3 dots) icon.

- From the popup menu, choose Auto Translate.

The Translate software will recognize when you start and finish speaking, allowing the other person to react without interacting with the iPhone.

How to Refresh a Webpage Quickly in Safari

Apple still provides a refresh symbol in the address bar that you can press to reload the currently viewed website. However, there is now another, less visible option to refresh web pages that you may find more convenient.

In Safari, a downward swipe on any webpage is all that is required to refresh it. This alternative to hitting the reload button is convenient if you like to maintain the address bar at the top of the screen, where tapping the reload icon might be inconvenient.

How to Change the Start Page and Background of Safari

- With iPhone or iPad, enter Safari.

- Tap the open tabs symbol in the Safari screen's bottom right corner.

- Press the Plus symbol in the bottom left corner to launch a new tab in the Tabs view.

- Scroll to the bottom of the Start Page and select the Edit button.

- Next to Use Start Page on All Devices, Turn on the button to sync your Start Page settings with additional devices linked to the same Apple ID.

- Control what appears on your Start Page by using the switches. In Safari, the topics on the front page, like Favorites, Frequently Visited, Shared with You, Privacy Report, Siri Suggestions, Reading List, and iCloud Tabs, are part of the options one can view.

- By pressing the large Plus icon, you can enable the Background image option and pick one of the available iOS wallpapers or create your own from your photographs. When you're finished, tap the X in the top-right corner of the menu card.

How to Make Use of Tab Groups in Safari

- Tap the Open Tabs icon in the bottom right corner of the screen to launch Safari.

- Tap or long-press the tab bar at the bottom of the screen in the center.

- Choose New Empty Tab Group. Alternatively, choose New Tab Group from X Tabs if you already have the tabs you wish to combine open.

- Enter a name for your Tab Group and then press Save.

- After you've made a Tab Group (or several), you may quickly switch between them by pressing the Tab bar in the open tabs view and selecting the one you want. When a Tab Group is selected, all open tabs will be immediately added to that group.

How to Use Siri

An update to Apple's voice assistant, Siri, has made it more context-aware, including support for offline requests and on-device processing.

Share Screen Using Siri

With Siri, you can now share your iPhone screen with your friends through a Message, including photos, websites, songs, or local weather reports.

To share any content, say "Hey Siri," then use the command, "Share this with [person]." Next, Siri will prompt you to ask, "Are you ready to send it?" Say yes/no; alternatively, add a remark to the message via the input box and tap Send.

If the content can't be shared directly, for instance, the weather forecast, the voice assistant will take a screenshot and send it. Simply use the command, "Share this with [person]," and Siri will capture the screenshot and approve the request.

Using Siri to Control HomeKit Devices

You can now use Siri to manage HomeKit devices at specific times.

For instance, if you wish to switch off your light bulb at 9:00 p.m., use the command, "Hey Siri, set the bulb to turn off at 9 p.m." the voice assistant will equally reply to geolocation commands; thus, you can say, "Hey Siri, switch off the lights when I'm away."

Suppose you ask the virtual assistant to control a HomeKit product this way. In that case, it'll create an automation in the Home app below the "Automation" tab. To erase an Automation in the Home app, just swipe leftwards across it and click on Delete.

In addition, HomeKit developers can include Siri support in their devices. However, Siri commands with 3rd-party devices require you to own a HomePod to route the command.

Through Siri integration, third-party HomeKit devices can be managed with Siri instructions by controlling devices, programming reminders, broadcasting messages, etc.

Activate Siri

- Head to Settings.

- Tap Siri and Search > Listen to enable the feature.

- After enabling Siri, just say "Hey Siri" to activate the voice assistant.

Activate Siri with Side Button

To activate Siri, pressing and holding the Side button for a few seconds (2–3) will be okay.

Exit Siri

When you're done with Siri and want to exit, simply swipe up from the bottom of the interface or press the side button to return to the Home screen.

Change Siri's Language

- Go to Settings.

- Swipe down and tap Siri and Search.

- Select Language.

- Pick a new language and tap Change Language to confirm your selection.

- Tap the "Hey Siri" toggle on Siri and the Search settings page to train Siri on the new language.

Using Siri Shortcuts

Siri Shortcuts lets you perform routine tasks speedily and with the applications you use with only a press or by asking Siri. Siri learns your routines across your apps. Siri then recommends a simple method to accomplish regular functions on the Lock screen or in Search. For instance, if you request news flash consistently on an app, Siri may recommend your preferred news.

To utilize a Siri Suggestion, press it on the lock screen. On the other hand, swipe down from the center of your screen to show Search; at that point, press the Siri Suggestion.

Adding Shortcuts to Siri

You can likewise run any shortcut by asking Siri.

Search for the "Add to Siri" button in your most-used apps and tap to include your very own expression, or then again go to Settings to find all shortcuts accessible.

Shortcuts that require an app to launch on your iPhone won't take a shot at HomePod and Apple Watch.

Adding Shortcuts from a Third-Party App

- Launch the third-party app and press Add to Siri.

- Tap (red icon). At that point, record a personal catchphrase that you'll tell Siri to run the Shortcut. Ensure that you record an easy expression that you'll recall.

- Tap "Done."

Adding Shortcut from Settings

- Launch the **Settings** > **Siri and Search**

- You'll see 3 proposed shortcuts. Tap All Shortcuts to see more actions from various apps.

- Tap Plus.

- To record a personal expression, tap (red icon). Then, attempt to record an easy expression that you'll recall.

- Tap "Done."

Delete a Shortcut/Change the Phrase

- Head to **Settings** > **Siri and Search** > **My Shortcuts**.

- To change the expression for the shortcut, tap the shortcut, and tap Re-Record Phrase.

- To erase a shortcut, swipe left over the shortcut and then press Delete. Alternatively, tap the shortcut and press Delete Shortcut.

A New Offline Siri Function

There is a new level of Siri operation in iOS 15 software for iPhones. This time, you do not require a Wi-Fi or cellular connection for Siri to function, as you can turn on the flight mode on the iPhone and still invoke Siri. However, some tasks may be limited compared to when connected to cellular or Wi-Fi networks. For example, easy tasks, such as setting the alarm or playing music, do not require internet connectivity. However, you'll still need an internet connection via Wi-Fi or cellular for Siri to carry out information-based requests, like weather updates.

CAMERA & PHOTOS

Camera Tools

To set your shot with an iPhone camera, use camera tools.

You may edit and improve your photograph by using options in your iPhone camera before shooting a snapshot. Turn on and off the flash, establish a timer, modify the focus and exposition of your camera, use the grid to straighten your shots, or apply a filter.

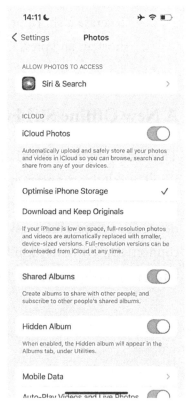

Turn the Flash on or off

If necessary, your iPhone camera is programmed to use the flash automatically. To regulate the flash manually before taking a photo, do this:

- Tap the Flash button to turn the automatic flash on or off on the iPhone XS, iPhone XR, and after. Tap the Flash button underneath the frame to choose Auto, On, or Off.

- Before the iPhone X click the Flash button, then select Auto, On, or Off.

Apply Filter on a Picture

To provide a color impact to your photo, use a filter. First, please choose Photo or Portrait mode, then do one of them:

- On the XS, XR, and later iPhone: Tap the button Controls Camera and tap the Filters button.

- Tap the filters button on the top of the screen for iPhone X and before.

- Move the filters left or right below the viewer to pre-see them; tap one for use.

Use Camera Timer

- Set a timer to make time for you to be in the shot.

- Tap the camera control button, tap on the Timer button, select 3s or 10s, then tap the Shutter button to start the timer on your iPhone XS, iPhone XR, etc.

- Hit Timer, choose 3s or 10s on iPhone X, and then tap Shutter to start the timer.

Take Live Photos

A live photograph, including audio, records everything that happens right before and after your picture. You capture a Live picture in the same way as a normal photo.

- In the photo, click on Photo mode.

- Ensure that Live Photo is enabled. When it's on, you notice the Live Photo button at the top of your camera. To turn on or off Live Photo, tap the Live Photo button.

- To capture a live picture, tap the Shutter button.

- Tap the picture at the bottom of the screen, and touch and hold the screen to play the live photo.

Take a Selfie

The front-facing camera can take a photo, portrait, or video record in Photo mode (on iPhone X and later).

- Switch to the front of your camera by tapping the back-end button of the Camera Chooser (depending on your model).

- Hold in front of you your iPhone.

Tip: Tap the arrows in the frame to widen the vision scope on iPhone 11, iPhone 12, and iPhone 13 devices.

- Tap on the shutter button or push the volume button to capture the shot or start recording.

Portrait Mode

You may use studio-quality lighting effects in your portrait mode shots on your iPhone 13Plus, iPhone X, and later. As a result, the subject is sharp in the viewfinder while the background is blurry.

The dial for portrait lighting effects is open on the lower of the frame, and Studio Light is chosen. The Flash button is in the top left of the screen, and the Camera Controls are in the top center, while the Portrait lighting intensity and depth control are controlled by buttons in the top right of the screen. The photo and video viewing button, the Take Photo button, and the Camera Chooser Back-Face button are at the bottom of the screen from left to right.

- Select portrait mode.

- Follow onscreen recommendations in the yellow Portrait Box to frame your subject.

- Drag the Lighting portrait control to select the lighting effect

- To take a shot, tap Shutter.

- You can delete the portrait mode effect after taking a photo in portrait mode if you don't like it. Tap Edit and select Portrait in the Photos app to turn on or off the shot.

Note: Night mode is enabled while taking a portrait mode with a wide (1x) lens on iPhone 13 Pro and iPhone 13 Pro Max.

Use Camera Live Text

The camera can copy and share text on iPhone XS, iPhone XR, and later, access webpages, create e-mails, and make calls from text within the camera frame.

- Open the camera and set the iPhone to display the text in the frame.

- Tap on the Live Text button after the yellow frame is displayed.

- Swipe or utilize grab points for text selection, and then do the following:

  ○ Copy text: To paste the text into an app like Notes or Messages.

  ○ Select All: Choose all of the frame's text.

- ○ Search: Search text on the internet.

- ○ Translate: Translate Text.

- ○ Share: Share AirDrop text, messages, email, or other modes available.

- Tap the URL, mobile number, or e-mail address on the screen to make a call, access a website or start an e-mail.

- To return to your camera, tap the Live Text On button.

Use Live Text to Interact with Photos

You can use Live text to copy and share text in a photo, translate languages, access the site, or make a call when you look at a photo in your Photos app. Visual Look Up can also identify, communicate and provide information on popular landmarks, art, plants, pets, etc., in your photographs.

Visual Look Up

Find out more about the famous monuments, plants, flowers, animals, and other objects in your images (the U.S. only).

- Open a full-screen photo, and the Visual Look Up button means that Visual Look Up information can be accessed for that image.

- Tap the Visual Look Up button or swipe to the photo.

- To see Siri Knowledge and more information about the object, tap the icon appearing in the photo or top of your photo information window.

- At the top of the screen, a picture is open. A dog and a Visual Lookup symbol are inside the shot. The lower half of the screen shows Siri's knowledge of the breed of dogs and similar web pictures.

Personalize Pictures Memories

In the Photos app, you may edit your memories to make them more personal. Try out memory mixes that allow you to apply various tracks with a corresponding photographic look. There are also new songs, memory titles can be edited, length changed, and photographs can be removed. The millions of songs accessible in the Apple Music collection enable Apple Music customers to add.

Add Memory Mix

Memory mixes are selected combinations of various melodies, pacings, and photographic images that modify the look and feel of a memory.

- Tap For you, then tap a player's memory.

- Tap the screen and press the Memory Mixes button.

- Swipe to examine various memory mixes on the left.

- Click the screen to apply Memory Mix.

Change Screen Brightness and Color

You can dim or brighten your display on an iPhone (dimming the screen extends battery life). You may manually or automatically modify the color and brightness of the screen through Dark Mode, True Tone, and Night Shift.

Manually Adjust the Screen Luminosity

To dim or lighten your iPhone screen, perform one of the following:

- Drag the Brightness button after opening the control center.

- Go to Settings > Display and Brightness, then shift the slider.

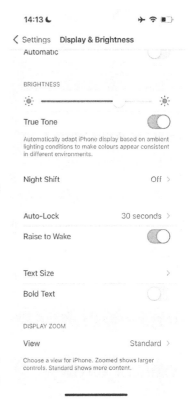

Automatically Change the Screen Brightness

IPhone adjusts screen brightness to current light conditions using the integrated ambient light sensor.

- Go to Settings > Accessibility.

- Tap Display and Size of text, then activate Auto-Brightness.

- Switch on or off Dark Mode

Dark Mode provides a dark color scheme for the full iPhone experience, ideal for low-light conditions. You may use your iPhone with Dark Mode without bothering the person beside you, for example, as you read in bed.

How to Drag and Drop Screenshot

Make a screenshot as you usually would by simultaneously tapping the Side and Volume Up buttons.

- Hold down the screenshot thumbnail in the bottom-left corner of the screen for a few seconds until the white frame around it disappears.

- Tap the app where you wish to use the screenshot with another finger. In this example, we will launch the Photos app, but you could also open Files, Messages, Mail, Notes, or something else.

- Navigate to the location where you wish to utilize the screenshot.

- Move the screenshot to the desired location, then release your finger to drop it in place.

Camera Interface

You can adjust many things before you take photos with the iPhone 13. These include:

- Video recording settings.

- Photos.

- Lighting settings.

- Sound settings.

- White balance.

To find these settings, open the Camera app, hit the Camera button, and select Camera Settings. Then choose from among the various camera settings:

This section can adjust how you want to capture photos, including the brightness, shutter speed, contrast, white balance, ISO, and exposure compensation. In addition, some settings will allow you to change your camera model.

When you're done, tap the Menu button in the top right corner of the iPhone 13's screen and tap Settings to go back to the iPhone 13's camera settings.

Camera Settings

iPhone cameras have several settings that can help you take a better-quality photo. You'll find these settings along the bottom of your camera screen.

ISO

This is the sensitivity setting of your camera. It's an indication of how sensitive the sensor is to light. The lower the number, the less sensitive it is. The lower the number, the greater the chance the photo will have noise, artifacts, or other problems. The best range to be in is 100–800, although it's recommended that you not shoot below 100.

Shutter Speed

This is the amount of time you give your camera to take a picture before taking the photo. To make a photo, you will choose the camera and then either press the shutter button halfway down or press and hold the button down for the length of time you want to wait before taking the photo. For example, if you want a 30-second exposure, hold the button down for 30 seconds. Shutter speed is displayed in either a digital stopwatch or in a count of frames, or if you choose, a range between zero and 30 seconds. When you're looking for the best shutter speed for your photo, experiment by adjusting it. As a rule of thumb, the fastest shutter speed is the best option when you take a picture.

Focus

The camera does this when it finds a subject to focus on. The focus is generally set at 1 of 2 points for both Manual or Auto focus modes. With a single focus point, your camera selects a focus point and places the image there. For a more precise focus, you can choose Manual Focus, which allows you to focus a picture manually. When you point the camera at a specific subject and press the shutter button, it will choose the closest and most focused subject.

Autofocus

This works automatically, with the camera focusing on subjects in the frame. If you're not too good at using autofocus, it often focuses on a person's face in a photo. With many other subjects, this can be a problem. Autofocus is an extra step you need to master, but it can lead to better pictures.

How to Use the Camera to Take Still Photos

- Open the camera app.

- Focus the lens of the theory on the object you want to capture.

- Then press the shutter button, and your photo will be saved immediately.

How to Use Live Focus

Live focus photography is a photography technique that produces photos with sharp, sharp, and crisp results. The camera app can adjust the background blur setting in real-time so that the image's background is always clear.

There are 4 different live focus features in the camera app, including:

- **Auto Focus (AF):** This feature uses autofocus technology to adjust the camera's focus in real-time.

- **Slow Focus (S):** When using this feature, the camera first takes a fast image and then waits several seconds for the subject to enter the frame.

- **Manual Focus (M):** It lets the user adjust the focus using the camera's ring.

It lets the user adjust the focus using the camera's ring. Focus Stacking (C): This feature allows users to take consecutive photos while focusing on different parts of a single subject.

Step 1: Select the Live Focus Mode

- Open the Camera app.

- Tap on the Live Focus icon.

Step 2: Pick the Live Focus Mode You Want to Use

- Position the object and press the shutter button.

How to Use Portrait Mode

- Open your camera.

- Search for portrait mode just above the shutter button.

- Then focus your camera on what you want to capture.

How to Take Panoramic Pictures

The first thing you do is unlock my phone and open up Photos. You can do that by tapping on the icon in the bottom-left.

You should see "Prano" in the upper right-hand corner in Photos. That's my default, and if you don't have that, you can press the little circle to the right of Pano or tap on the word pano in the upper right-hand corner.

And that's about it. Then press "Take Panorama," which is on the screen's bottom-left.

You'll see the usual instructions: press the shutter when the camera app says to. You'll have the option of zooming and shooting and all the other camera settings.

You can then save the picture.

How to Take Screenshot

To take a screenshot, just press the Sleep/Wake button and the Home button at the same time. This will save the screenshot into the iPhoto library.

You can also capture a screenshot of your iPhone or iPad screen using the same button combination or even just double-tap the Home button to take a screen snapshot.

You can also take screenshots of a live video by pressing the power button and the Volume down button at the same time.

Take a Screenshot With Gestures

Your device allows you to take a screenshot with a gesture. With a double press of the sleep/wake button or by using the side button + Shift button, your iPhone will instantly capture all visible elements of the screen. If you want to take a screen capture of just a section of your screen, press and hold your finger in that area, and your iPhone will automatically take a screenshot of that part of the screen.

Using Screen Recorder

The screen recorder is straightforward to use. A dedicated icon on the screen can record all your screen activities. You don't need to download and install any software. Instead, just tap the icon, and the screen is recorded in 4K quality (which you need to be connected to the Internet). After recording, you can replay the video, share it on the social networking site, and upload it for sharing and making presentations.

How to Record Screen on iPhone 13 Series

Just go to the Settings app and tap on Screen Time. Next, tap on Screen Time and tap on the Record button. Here, you will see the option to start or stop the recording. You can also delete the recording if required.

Also you can do the same by going to the Control Center and tapping the Rec button. The screen will record in 4K. You will be able to record for up to 30 minutes.

How to Take Videos

- Open the camera app.

- Just above the shutter button, you will see "video" click on it.

- When pressing the circle icon (shutter button) will begin to display a little dot in between.

- Then your video has started recording.

- When you are done, press the icon with the dotted red in between to save the video.

- The video will be saved immediately.

How to Scan Qr Code with Your Camera

QR (QR bar code) or Quick Response bar code is a data matrix code and a type of 2D bar code. It is a popular and universal encoding standard used to create links between products. The symbol of QR is a square QR code.

A QR code can be used on a phone, tablet, or any other device, which has a camera to recognize QR codes.

Some apps support QR codes, including the camera app of your iPhone. You can take pictures with your camera app and scan a QR code. To use the QR code scanner in the camera app, follow the steps below:

- **Step 1:** Open the camera app on iPhone 13 Pro Max. On iPhone XR, there will be no way to open the camera. Therefore, you can only view images and videos on iPhone XS, XS Max, and XR.

- **Step 2:** From the top row of the camera app, tap the Scanner icon. You will see that the bottom row has 5 options:

  - Use Photo Library

  - Use All Schemes

  - Custom Scan

  - QR Code Scanner

  - All Photos.

- **Step 3:** Open the Camera app to select the QR code mode. Use the Photo Library to open the QR code mode.

- **Step 4:** From the menu bar on the camera's left side, tap the QR Code option, then tap either QR Code.

If the camera already scanned the QR Code, it will appear on the screen. You can then edit the QR code. Tapping the QR Code option again will display the QR code reader, a bar code scanner. The QR code reader can scan all kinds of documents, text, QR codes, and bar codes.

The QR code scanner will likely be the next best fingerprint scanner.

- **Step 5:** From the QR code reader app, you can edit the bar code, such as edit QR code or remove it, and create new QR codes.

How to Use Picture-In-Picture

Picture-in-picture on iPhone 13 has its place in the user interface. It allows you to watch 2 different videos at the same time. So you could watch a movie, play a video game or do anything else you want while being able to watch TV.

Using picture-in-picture on iPhone 13 allows you to: watch movies while being able to talk on the phone. Watch movies while being able to listen to the radio. Watch movies while doing other stuff on your iPhone. Watch videos while doing other tasks on your iPhone.

- To use picture-in-picture on iPhone 13, all you need to do is to tap on the Settings icon on the side of the display. Next, tap on the Picture-in-Picture option.

- With picture-in-picture turned on, you'll see that it's now the first option in the settings menu for picture-in-picture. If you turn off picture-in-picture, you'll have to turn it on again.

- Tap on picture-in-picture, and then tap on the blue arrow to enable picture-in-picture.

- Once you're done, picture-in-picture will be enabled on your iPhone. You'll now see that the screen will be split into 2 parts. To start using picture-in-picture, you'll need to drag the image or video you want to watch up to the top-left portion of the screen. Once you've dragged the video there, you'll be able to see the video with the speaker icon in the top-left corner of the screen.

- Next, you'll want to add an audio source from the music app. The audio can come from the phone's speaker or another connected speaker. To add an audio source, tap on the speaker icon.

- The speaker icon will then become blue, and you'll see the speaker icon appear in the top-left corner of the screen. Now, just tap on it to start the audio.

- Also, you'll be able to control the audio volume, so you don't want to miss any important parts of the video or audio. In the next section, we'll explain how to control the volume.

How to Control Volume

- If you're watching a video on the iPhone and want to control the volume, you'll need to tap on the video. Next, you'll tap on the volume slider.

- The slider will display the current volume level on the screen. You can control the volume by using the slider to turn it up or down.

That's it! That's how to make picture-in-picture on iPhone.

The Cinematic Mode Will Allow You to Shoot Movies Like a Pro

Apple has replenished the cameras on the new iPhone 13 series with an impressive cinematic mode. It seems that with the improvement of portable cameras, users can become a new tool for shooting video. Furthermore, the new audio recorders can completely change the look of the video taken from the iPhone, and the iPhone 13 won't disappoint in this regard. In the past, Apple has provided various tools to make the best home movies. For example, slow motion mode allows users to shoot high-definition video at high frame rates, allowing the user to shoot and watch epic videos at low speeds. While under the hood, Apple has also improved cloud-based image capture and low-light performance. Taken together, these new Apple features are even more beautiful.

The current model, Cinema Mode, changes the game when it comes to video games. In this way, the iPhone combines artificial intelligence with real-world techniques used by directors to change focus and create intense depth while shooting automatically. When the subject is seen in the picture, the detail gradually changes to point naturally to the beholder's eye. The iPhone will focus on the new person if this object looks away or at another person on the set. The user also can manually change the focus by selecting the fact that the iPhone will detect while shooting. This may be useful if the shooter wants the viewer's objects to be more detailed. Also, cinema mode records in Dolby Vision HDR, allowing you to improve colors and details and further enhance the recording.

Cinematic as a Professional

These features are available on the iPhone 13, but the iPhone 13 Pro gets something more special. While it looks like a Pro, users can shoot from a wide, telephoto, or TrueDepth camera in cinematic mode. Although in-depth adjustments are made in real-time, according to Apple, the process is quite complicated. It seems that the iPhone 13 and iPhone 13 Pro use high-quality, in-depth data between the subject and the camera to calculate the focus accurately switching locations. This data is constantly updated at 30 frames per second - this is close to the standard frame rate for movies. The ability for the iPhone to decide where to look is provided by a neural motor included in the A15 Bionic chip.

Cinema mode changes the game in terms of mobile video. Perhaps the ability to shoot Dolby Vision HDR and produce cinematic effects now is a useful tool for video shooters. As interest in video capture on a mobile device increases, Apple's new camera enhancements will likely become increasingly popular among iPhone 13 and iPhone 13 Pro users.

The iPhone 13 features 120Hz displays, longer battery life, and more.

Apple has provided some exciting features for this generation. As with the iPad Pro, the device's 13 high-speed upgrades increase the frame rate from the usual 60Hz to 120Hz. While this requires internet access, it's much easier to keep up with Twitter and games than it was on past iPhones.

Then there is the camera. The iPhone 13 and 13 Mini have a few welcome updates. The 12-megapixel main screen is the main screen of the iPhone with a dual-screen of 1.7 microns and provides an additional 47% of brightness. Apple also has a new 12-megapixel ultra-wide camera with similar upgrades and Sensor-Shift technology to improve focus and stability in all shooting conditions. Next is the iPhone 13 Pro camera configuration. The 77mm telephoto lens improves portrait photography and light sensitivity for wide and ultra-wide cameras. Also, new this year, the macro mode for the ultra-wide camera was a new year—the first for any iPhone.

Let's start summarizing. Apple's latest A15 Bionic chipset power all 4 phones. Apple advertises this as 30% faster than its competitors. It has 6 core GPUs, 4 GPU cores, and Apple has improved its neural engine for better machine learning functions. Interestingly, the iPhone 13 Pro and 13 Pro Max get a faster 5-core GPU, which is not available in the usual 13 and 13 Mini. There's also better battery life. The iPhone 13 Mini and 13 Pro should get 1.5 hours of extra battery life compared to their predecessors and 2.5 additional hours on the Pro Max.

Apple iPhone 13: Camera and Camera Features

Until last year, the standard and maximum versions of the iPhone had no noteworthy differences, except for a larger display and a larger capacity battery. Along with the main camera improvements, the iPhone 12 Pro Max also had a better telephoto lens that transmits more light and a 2.5x magnification instead of a 2x in the standard Pro. This time Apple has also made the same camera improvements to the iPhone 13 Pro. The standard iPhone 13 also gets improved cameras, but not to the same extent as the Pro series (obviously). The 12MP primary camera has a larger sensor that saves up to 47% more light. Like the Pro model, the iPhone 13 also gets image stabilization with a sensor-shift.

The ultra-wide camera on the iPhone 13 has also improved and now takes better photos in low light. The front camera of the selfie has 12 MP. There are Apple HDR algorithms to optimize photos clicked from cameras on the device.

The iPhone 13 can shoot movie clips that can change focus depending on the elements present in the frame. Apple calls this cinematic mode. The cameras on the 3 devices can shoot up to 4K video at 60 frames per second. The iPhone was one of the best video capture devices, and only this year has it become the best. Deep Fusion and the ability to shoot HDR video are also present.

OTHER IPHONE 13 FEATURES

Design

Apple will continue to offer 4 iPhones in 2021. Without resizing, you will imagine the 5.4-inch iPhone mini, the 6.1-inch inexpensive iPhone, the 6.1-inch Pro model, and the 6.7-inch Pro Max model. Some people said the iPhone 12 mini sales needed to be more, yet Apple is still developing the iPhone 13 mini, even if it can account for only 10% of the total production of the iPhone 13.

Apple engineers believe the 2021 iPhones are the "S" type of the 2020 models. However, Apple had used the "S" nomenclature for ages when iPhone models introduced more minor upgrades.

The novel iPhones come with similar dimensions as the iPhone 12 models, and the thickness is anticipated to increase by 0.26mm. The iPhone 13 models will continue to be a little thicker because of the bigger batteries.

The standard model of the iPhone 13 could see the lenses diagonally rather than vertically by installing a dual-lens camera. This is not completely clear what the gadget's benefits will have been determined to give similar wide and ultra-wide lenses. It has a lot of modifications in stock, such as optical image maintenance for wide lenses that may require relocation.

The iPhone 13 Pro models come in 0.2 mm thick, to accommodate a bigger battery, with a heftier rear camera, permitting rendering images. You may need a larger camera unit to stabilize the sensor-shift, and it is the identical dimension as the rear camera unit from the iPhone 12 Pro Max.

It comes with a bigger camera size than the iPhone 13 Pro shown in the pictures of the iPhone 12 Pro. in the case of the iPhone 13 Pro, which has been conspicuous with a bigger camera. The iPhone 13 models can likewise have strong magnets on the inside and an unlikely matte color on the outside. And it has been said that future iPhones will be replaced by a matte black color that can substitute the gray space with a novel stainless steel cover that decreases stains and fingerprints.

It is available in the pink shade of the standard iPhone 13.

Display

The iPhone 13 series will be accessible in 3 different screen size selections, just like last year. The iPhone 13 mini retains the same 5.4-inch screen, though the iPhone 13 and iPhone 13 Pro come in at 6.1 inches. The iPhone 13 Pro Max comes in a 6.7-inch display as that of the iPhone 12 Pro Max.

All 4 phones come with Super Retina XDR OLED technology. The non-Pro models will be up to 800 nits of brightness, and the iPhone 13 Pro max and iPhone 13 Pro can dial up to 1000 nits. Apple also says the latest show technology is more efficient.

Apple says that the iPhone 13 Pro and iPhone 13 Pro Max will feature a ProMotion show. This means that 2 phones can lock their screens up to 120 Hz or 10 GHz. This range will help make the content you view more sensitive as iOS adapts the refresh rate to whatever you are doing.

Apple is also working with developers to enhance their applications and games for 120Hz applications.

Cameras and Cinematic Mode Video

Apple has added a major camera upgrade for the iPhone 13. Non-professional models have a new 12-megapixel ultra-wide sensor that delivers 47% more light. The 12 MP main wide-angle camera has optical image stabilization, a feature previously limited to the iPhone 12 Pro Max. This will help iPhone 13 and iPhone 13 mini to take beautiful photos in multiple lighting conditions.

The iPhone 13 Pro and iPhone 13 Pro Max can receive ultra-wide autofocus and a novel phone lens with 3x optical zoom. All 3 cameras also support night mode. The ultra-wide camera will similarly capture macro photography at near to 2cm, which will enhance the Pro model's photo capabilities.

With each new iPhone, you also get a photographic style that gives your personal preference for your photos in real-time. It's more than just a filter; it uses the correct corrections for different scenes to produce the best photos.

The 4 iPhone 13 models come with a cinematic mode that gives the best superior cinematography to Dolby Vision HDR videos. A requirement of the popularity of cinematic mode is its ability to dynamically change the focus and follow the subject of your video. If the subject is moving, the focus will also move. If a person is avoiding, the focus shifts to where the subject is looking. Just tap where you want to focus and then tap again to lock in focus.

The iPhone 13 Pro and iPhone 13 Pro Max will similarly shoot videos in ProRes format, opening plenty of professional-quality editing capabilities. Note, however, that 1080P covers the 128 GB version of the iPhone 13 Pro and Pro Max for ProRes video; 4 K ProRes support superior storage options.

iPhone 13 Spec

A15 Processor

The new iPhone 13 is built around the A15 Bionic System-on-a-Chip (SoC), Apple's best chip when it was introduced. It is built on a 5 nm process with 6 cores. The iPhone 13 boasts 2 new Firestorm high-power cores, while the other 4 Icestorm cores are more efficient than earlier versions. A neural engine advancement (NPU) powers a machine-learning app for the iPhone's software (iOS) live text feature and speech recognition on the Siri device.

SoC, RAM, and Storage

Every year Apple gives the iPhone an internal update using the latest mobile platform, and this year is no different. The iPhone 13 gets Apple's A15 Bionic chipset based on a 5-nm manufacturing process. Following the history of Apple chips, the A15 Bionic is one of the most powerful smartphone chipsets that can run anything you throw at it. Be it the most challenging game or a 4K video rendering, thanks to the A15 iPhone 13 chipset, you can do it all without a hitch.

It's not just the raw chipset's performance. Apple software is very well optimized to work with embedded hardware because Apple manufactures both items. This allows you to use the device smoothly and smoothly. Although the A15 Bionic will be based on the same 5-nm design as last year's A14 Bionic, it brings some notable features related to the performance of batteries. The A14 Bionic was already a powerful manufacturer, and the A15 Bionic only relies on it and further strengthens its leadership.

Apple never discloses the RAM capacity on the new iPhone explicitly. However, like the iPhone 12, the iPhone 13 also has 4GB of RAM. In terms of storage, the iPhone 13 starts at 128 GB as the base version, followed by 256 and 512 GB. After years of user requests, Apple has finally increased storage in the base version to 128 GB. Suppose you shoot a lot of 4K 60 frames per second video on your iPhone and use it as your main media machine. In that case, you'll appreciate the extra storage.

Small Size

With a 6.1 inch diagonal display, the iPhone 13 maintains the smaller size of the iPhone 12. The iPhone 13 Mini has a 5.4 inch diagonal display for an even smaller size. The iPhone 13 models pack more into a smaller volume.

Portable Design

Although there have been rumors of the Lighting connector disappearing, it is still in the iPhone 13 phone.

The handy iPhone can be charged wirelessly using Qi-based wireless charging and MagSafe accessories.

USB-C Is Not Available

Apple will not switch from iPhone Lightning to USB-C; Apple wants to avoid switching to USB-C since it is an exposed connector with less waterproof protection than Lightning.

Apple touts the superiority of Lightning cables compatible with accessories designed for iPhone (MFi) software, which is not possible with USB-C.

It is expected that the iPhone 13 and forthcoming iPhones will still use the Lightning ports till MagSafe accessories become accepted enough to use in a portable iPhone design.

No Touch ID

During the development of the iPhone 13, Apple tested a touch screen reader named Touch ID, which will do a better job of reading the biometric information that Apple has used since the release of the iPhone X in flagship devices, thus enabling dual biometric functionality.

Unfortunately, the iPhone 13 will not have a Touch ID fingerprint sensor.

Apple will continue to focus only on Face ID.

120Hz ProMotion Display

Before the release of the iPhone 12, some innovations recommended that high-end iPhone 12 models have a 120Hz ProMotion display. The news cycle revealed that this feature was delayed till 2021 because of battery issues.

The 120Hz video rate speed on the iPhone called Pro Motion. 2 models of the 2021 iPhone can use OLED show with low-power LTPO rear technology, paving the way for 120Hz upgrade speeds.

Since many apps don't support the 120Hz up date rate, you may not see an advantage.

Always On Display

The iPhone 13's Always-On Display allows some data, such as time to be displayed on the locked screen of the iPhone even when it is turned off.

Again, messages appear, but the screen does not fully illuminate.

Note: This mode does affect battery life.

Wi-Fi 6E and 5G Chip

The iPhone 13's 5G capability means faster data downloads and connections.

The iPhone 13 models support Wi-Fi 6E, which gives Wi-Fi 6 specifications and capabilities in the 6GHz band. Wi-Fi 6 offers higher presentation, lesser latency, and quicker data speeds. The extra range of Wi-Fi 6E gives more bandwidth above the present 2.4 and 5GHz Wi-Fi bands.

Larger Batteries

The iPhone 13 models have bigger batteries that can lead to better battery life. Apple has created an innovative space-saving design, like incorporating a SIM card into the motherboard and lowering the former optical module's thickness to give the battery more space.

The iPhone 13 comes with 3227 mAh battery. The A15 chip introduces additional enhancements for battery efficiency.

25W Power Adapter

iPhone 13 models can accelerate charging speed by supporting a 25W power converter. The iPhone 12 model support quick charging, but was limited to 20W maximum charging power.

Apple will likewise give a novel 25-watt adapter that will come into sale with newer iPhone models.

1 TB Increased Storage

The iPhone 13 model comes with up to 1TB of storage space compared to 512GB maximum storage in iPhone 12 models.

iPhone 13 and iOS 15

The best features of iOS 15 include FaceTime updates that allow you to watch videos and share content with others, a new Focus mode for managing messages, and improved Maps, Messages, Wallet, Weather, and other built-in apps.

iPhone 13 Perspective

Much of the focus of the iPhone 13 is on the cameras and the A15 Bionic chip. These are all notable updates. The iPhone 13 offers a lot more than its predecessor.

Pro models have a 120Hz ProMotion display, which will help iOS 15 look exceptionally sleek. All 4 models have excellent optical stabilization.

Battery and Charging

The device has the same 20W fast charging technology from last year that can charge your iPhone up to 50% in 30 minutes. However, the charger is not included and must be purchased separately. Apple introduced MagSafe charging with the iPhone 12 series and it has also made its way to the iPhone 13 series. Unfortunately, MagSafe has no new charging speed improvements and is still limited to the same 15W power as last year. MagSafe can also be used to attach other accessories.

5G and Connectivity

Last year, Apple introduced the iPhone 5G capabilities with the iPhone 12 series. Of course, the iPhone 13 also connects 5G and is truly a global phone for network and bandwidth support. The iPhone 13 supports all relevant 5G bands worldwide, so you don't have to worry about compatibility. You get support for both sub-6 GHz and mmWave 5G.

Software

IOS 15 also improves how you display your notifications by grouping them based on the apps that send them. Apple has also introduced various focus modes to help you not be distracted during the day. The camera app is also new, with live text support that can copy text from your photos, and you can even drag copied text to the Notes app or any other app on iOS 15. Siri has made some improvements, Safari, weather, and search in focus too. You can also view the privacy reports on iOS 15 that show which app had access to what information on your phone.

Security and Additional Services

Apple has abandoned TouchID on the iPhone in favor of Face ID, and that's what you'll get on the iPhone 13. There have been rumors of a built-in fingerprint scanner that appeared in the iPhone 13 series, but that, unfortunately, turned out to be false. So instead, face ID sensors are in the notch above the display, this time thankfully smaller. The clipping houses an infrared camera and a point projector that works in tandem to create a 3D model of your face scanned to unlock the phone.

Design

You will learn all about the hidden features coming in iOS 15 and all the essential information you need to use an iPhone device running iOS 15 properly. So, we will dive into the steps and knowledge to make you an expert on iOS 15.

A New Safari Layout

The Safari browser app on iOS 15 has a new look and URL address bar layout. Initially, in the late iOS software versions, the Safari browser app had its URL address bar on top of the display. But this time, on iOS 15, the URL address bar in the Safari app has its bar at the bottom of the screen, unlike on iOS 14.

The good thing is you can revert this change in the Safari app right in the Settings app of your iPhone.

- **Step 1:** Navigate to and launch the Settings app on your iPhone.

- **Step 2:** Scroll down on the screen of the Settings app to locate the option with the "Safari" tag on it.

- **Step 3:** Tap-open the section to take you to the settings section for your Safari browser app.

- **Step 4:** Scroll down till you get to the section tagged "Tabs."

- **Step 5:** That section has 2 tab bar options with sample image previews for check options: "Tab Bar" and "Single Bar."

- **Step 6:** Select the Single bar options button to revert your Safari's URL address to the top position as in the previous iOS versions.

If you follow the earlier-stated steps, you will successfully revert the URL address type box to the initial position on the Safari app, which is at the top of the homepage. Aside from the URL address layout change, there are other changes, such as the tab multitasking preview outlet in the app. The icon for accessing tabs on Safari is the same as on the previous iOS, with the side-by-side 2-tabs icon at the bottom-right corner of the screen. The new layout of the tabs is in a full page-to-page grid view, unlike the sort of slideshow tabs view on the previous iOS versions, enabling you to view each page correctly. Swipe leftwards on any tab you wish to discard to close it. Long-press on the "Done" button in the bottom-right corner of the screen to close all the tabs at once.

You can reverse the closed tabs if you wish to when you long-press on the plus icon (+) at the bottom-left corner of the tab multitasking preview screen, the same as closing all tabs. And after 1 second or 2, the recently closed tabs will pop up on the left of the screen for selection.

Live Text

Live Text on iOS 15 is one of the most impressive features among the new features on the new operating system. It enables you to copy the text on a picture, whether an instantly-taken picture or a picture you had on the iPhone before you updated it to the latest iOS 15 software version. In the feature, you can directly copy the text on any photographed or downloaded image into the iPhone's clipboard or search the internet to get information about the text in the picture. The steps for using Live Text on iPhones running iOS 15 are listed below.

- **Step 1:** Open any image of your choice in the Photos app or any medium that contains text, even on social media.

- **Step 2:** Long-press on the text area till a rectangular panel appears above the text with 'Copy,' 'Select all,' 'Translate,' and 'Look up' options.

The 'Copy' option on the panel automatically copies the text into your iPhone's clipboard for pasting into another app, such as the Notes app. The 'Select all' option works by selecting all the text in the image, including copying or looking up the text on the internet. The "Look up" option enters the text into an internet search to determine details about the text, such as its meaning, translation, history, or location if it is a company name. After choosing the "Look up" option, the underlying information on the following screen is Siri suggestions, apart from the information you get on Google search.

Aside from already-taken photos, you can utilize the Live Text feature even before taking any photo containing text, just as you did with the already-shot image.

The HashTag in the Notes App

A new feature in the Notes app on iOS 15 allows you to easily track your notes in the app. When writing a text in the Notes app in iOS 15, you can now include a hashtag behind a text, and it will automatically turn into a highlighted text with a different color.

To do this:

- Scroll to the bottom of the screen of the Notes app where you want to find the text.

- There, you'll find a menu at the bottom of the screen containing the list of texts or notes with a hashtag (#).

- Tap on the exact one you inputted earlier to access its contents instantly.

- After you tap on any hashtag text, the screen that follows display the list of hashtags, and there's a complete menu of all of them when you swipe to the left end of the display. It is especially beneficial to tag a note for any emergency quickly.

Background Sounds

Aside from utilizing the "Hearing" feature icon (symbolized by an ear) on the Control Center or AirPods Pro's "Live Listen" feature. The "Live Listen" feature for the AirPods Pro gives a different function if it is not connected to the iPhone. You can tap on it to play background sounds without downloading one, such as the rainfall sound.

- **Step 1:** Slide down on the top-right corner of the iPhone's screen to access the control menu.

- **Step 2:** Tap open the hearing icon (with an ear symbol).

- **Step 3:** Inside the hearing icon is a list of options for Background Sounds, a slider volume control, and the "Live Listen" feature. Click on the "Background Sounds" option to select the sound you need.

- **Step 4:** The screen automatically returns to the icon's home display after you select a sound. Slide right on the volume control to increase the sound to the extent you want the background sound to play.

New Slideshow Feature

In your Photos app, you have a brand new feature on the memories slideshow to add music files and different filters you want on the slideshow rather than a static control on the previous software versions.

   Below is how to set up the Memories slide show on an iOS 15 iPhone.

- **Step 1:** Right inside your Photos app on your iPhone, access the memories tab or folder direction to start up a slideshow as usual on the prior version of software on the iPhone.

- **Step 2:** Tap on the music icon at the screen's bottom left corner to access a different setup for the "Memories" slideshow.

- **Step 3:** On the next screen, you will find 2 icons: the Music icon with a plus (+) sign on it; and the Filter icon (made up of 3 overlapping circles). Tap the music icon to add music from your music library or Apple Music.

- **Step 4:** After you've made your selection, click "Done" in the top-right corner of the screen to add the music file to the slideshow.

- **Step 5:** On the screen where you tapped on the music icon with a plus (+) sign, you can tap on the filter icon (made up of 3 overlapping circles) to add any filter you want on the slideshow.

- **Step 6:** Click "Done" in the top-right corner of the screen after making your filter selection.

Other

What Is Live Text Used for?

Live Text is a feature on the iPhone 13 that helps identify the text in images after doing that. After doing that, the user can then copy the text and paste the text into another app. They can translate the text if it's in a foreign language and can search for more information about the text on the internet.

One of the most prominent uses of this feature is that it helps to copy text automatically without typing it manually. So, for example, users can take a photo of a physical letter, use live text to copy its content, then paste the text into an email rather than manually copying it.

Live Text has numerous uses since it can automatically search for a text and translate it to other languages.

For example, you can use Live Text on a book in the Camera app or a photo of a book in the Photos app to check the internet for more information about that book.

If you're in a foreign country and see a signboard in a foreign language, you can snap the picture and run it through Live Text.

Create Contact Account

- To add an account, move to **Settings** > choose **Contacts** > **Accounts** > click Add Account > Other.

- Select Add LDAP Account or Add CardDAV Account (as applicable to your company), then input your server and account details.

Create Calendar Account

- Move to **Settings** > choose Calendar > **Accounts** > Add Account to add an account.

- Select Other and then one of the following:

  - Include calendar account: Touch Add CalDAV Account, then input your server and account details.

  - Subscribe to iCal calendars (.ics): Touch Add Subscribed Calendar, then input the URL for the .ics file you wish to subscribe to or load in a .ics file from Mail.

Glossary

- **Apple ID:** This is an email address registered with Apple.

- **Apple Store:** This retail and online powerhouse sells Apple products.

- **Apple TV:** Apple's original Mac OS X Tiger-based living room set-top box designed to buy media from the iTunes Store or stream it from Mac or Windows iTunes.

- **Bookstore:** Bookstore allows you to buy, browse, search, and buy eBooks.

- **Gmail:** Web designed for email services.

- **Google:** This provides internet search but also provides Youtube and other apps.

- **GPRS:** This is data networking.

- **iCloud:** It's as an Apple's online service that is used for replacing MobileMe.

- **iMessage:** This SMS or MMS is used for sending free text and multimedia messages from one iOS device to another over cellular and Wi-Fi networks.

- **iOS:** iOS is an Apple mobile operating iPad that powers Apple products.

- **iPod touch G3:** Apple's 3rd generation iPod touch added more RAM and faster CPU and GPU. Released September 9, 2009.

- **iPod touch G4:** Apple's 4th generation iPod touch, added a Retina Display, front and back-facing cameras with FaceTime, and a gyroscope.

- **iTunes:** This is Mac and Windows software used to activate or sync iPhone

- **Photos:** Handle the camera.

- **Personal Hotspot:** It allows sharing cellular data over a Wi-Fi connection with up to 6 additional devices.

- **Photo Stream:** Stores photos for up to 30 days.

- **Ping:** It lives inside iTunes on Mac and is hooked up on Twitter.

- **Private API:** Apple will reject any app that uses a Private API.

- **QuickTime:** It is used to play movies and other videos on iOS.

- **Respring:** Relaunching iPhone, iPod touch, or iPad's Springboard. Jailbreak apps use it after installation or changes to Springboard.

- **Safari:** Safari is an Apple web browser for Mac OS X and iOS.

- **SDK:** (Software Developers Kit) is a set of tools, including API, frameworks, interface elements, etc., used to create software, i.e., apps.

- **Web Kit:** This is an open-source HTML browser.

- **Wi-Fi:** Wireless networking.

Made in the USA
Las Vegas, NV
02 November 2023

80133171R00090